PEACE OR PANIC

God's Time Frame in Bible Prophecy

MICHAEL BAKER

ACW Press
Phoenix, Arizona 85013

Except where otherwise indicated all Scripture quotations are taken from the Holy Bible, New International Version®. Copyright © 1973, 1978, 1984 by the International Bible Society. Used by permission of Zondervan Publishing House. The "NIV" and "New International Version" trademarks are registered in the United States Patent and Trademark Office by International Bible Society.

Verses marked KJV are taken from the King James Version of the Bible.

The Mishnah references used in this book, God's Time Frame, come from the Art Scroll Mishnah Series, published by Mesorah Publications, LTD Brooklyn New York. See the bibliography for more information on this publication.

Peace or Panic
Copyright ©2002 Michael Baker
All rights reserved

Cover Design by Alpha Advertising
Interior design by Pine Hill Graphics

Packaged by ACW Press
5501 N. 7th Ave., #502
Phoenix, Arizona 85013
www.acwpress.com
The views expressed or implied in this work do not necessarily reflect those of ACW Press. Ultimate design, content, and editorial accuracy of this work is the responsibility of the author(s).

Library of Congress Cataloging-in-Publication Data

Baker, Michael S.
    Peace or panic? : G-d's time frame in Bible prophecy
/ by Michael S. Baker. -- 1st ed.
    p. cm.
    Includes bibliographical references and index.
    ISBN: 1-892525-75-5

    1. Bible--Prophecies. 2. Fasts and feasts in the
Bible--Typology. 3. Fasts and feasts--Judaism.
4. Eschatology--Biblical teaching. I. Title.

BS647.2.B35 2002   236
                      QBI02-200224

All rights reserved. No part of this book may be reproduced, stored in a retrieval system, or transmitted in any form or by any means–electronic, mechanical, photocopying, recording, or otherwise–without prior permission in writing from the copyright holder except as provided by USA copyright law.

Printed in the United States of America.

ACKNOWLEDGMENTS

I wish to thank the following for their patience with me while I was working on the manuscript. A special thanks to Ed Schroeder, who talked me into teaching the Jewish feasts and festivals in our adult Sunday school class at Meadview Baptist Church. It took me sixteen months to go through the feasts during Sunday School, and most of my notes for this class were used in God's Time Frame. I would also like to thank Ed and Wanda Schroeder for their encouragement over morning coffee and through the many attacks of the devil while I was writing this book. I would also like to thank John Schroeder for his help in getting me through learning a new computer and designing my web page.

The members of Meadview Baptist Church were a great support team. Thank you for all of your prayers and the great potlucks. Fran Wilson, the prayer leader for the church, was a great encouragement for me to press on with the book. I wish to thank the Lowdens for support and a place to stay while I was in the middle of the craziness.

I also wish to thank Chuck Dean and his team at ACW Press for their patience and skill in turning a new concept into something that will have an impact on the Church for many years to come.

The Lord was working on this project as well. Every time a question would come up about the Bible or Jewish law, the answer would be found within a day or so. The needed resource material would always show up at just the right time and give more insight to the word of God.

CONTENTS

Introduction	7
The Hebrew Calendar	9
The Hebrew Day	9
Watches of the Night	
The Hebrew Calendars	12
The Mishnah	13
The New Year's	15
The Civil Calendar	17
The Religious Calendar	19
The Sabbath	23
Most Important Day	23
Sabbath Laws	24
The Sabbath in the Home	28
High Sabbath	29
The Earth's Sabbath	30
The Year of Jubilee	31
One Thousand Years are as One Day.	33
The Spring Feasts	39
Pilgrimage Feasts	39
Passover and Unleavened Bread	41
The Passover	41
The Feast of Unleavened Bread	46
The Haggadah	46
The Four Symbols	50
Feast of Firstfruits	53
Feast of Pentecost	55
The Day of Atonement?	59

Fall Feasts — 61
- Repentance — 63
- The Three Books? — 65
- The Watchman — 66
- The New Moon Festival — 69
- The Feast of Trumpets — 71
- The Day of Atonement — 76
  - The Laws of Yom Kippur — 77
  - Jesus Establishes His Residence — 78
  - The High Priest Atones for His House — 80
  - The High Priest's Portion — 82
  - The Upper Chamber — 83
  - The Mount of Olives — 85
  - The Altar — 86
  - The Scapegoat — 87
  - The King's Household — 88
  - Guards Falling in Fear — 90
  - The Road to Emmaus — 91
  - Cooking a Feast — 99
- Feast of Tabernacles — 102
  - A Succah — 105
  - The Light of the World — 106
  - The House of the Water Pouring — 109
  - The Four Species — 111

Other Feasts — 113
- Chanukah — 113
- Purim — 118

A Thousand Years Are as One Day — 121
- Biblical Account — 121
- The Puzzle Border — 122
- Where Are We Now? — 149

Appendix A — 151

Appendix B — 158

Appendix C — 160

Bibliography — 161

Scripture — 174

Mishnah — 176

Glossary — 177

INTRODUCTION

A left turn at a red light in April 1983 put me less than a mile from my home in Ontario California. I was facing a multitude of problems, from my mother being very sick with cancer to the possibility of being thrown out of my new home, due to my escrow not closing. These were just a few of the problems.

Out of my mouth came something like this, "Is there really a God? I have to know the truth." An audible voice said, "What do you want!" Startled, I looked behind the seat of the truck; no one was there. Someone had to have hitched a ride because the voice came from behind me. I turned around while driving to look in the truck bed, and no one was there. With my mind racing, I looked behind the seat again and no one was there.

My life was changed forever. For some unknown reason, I knew the answers to my questions were to be found in the Bible. What should I do, now that God is real to me?

I had just moved into my new home, and I was in the market for a brand-new, top-of-the-line television. The computer industry was very good to me at this time. With a little pride and my new computerized television, I had to program in every single television channel in the Southern California area, including TBN, channel 40. I watched TBN for three days after I heard the voice of God in my truck and accepted Jesus as my Lord and Savior.

The years following this experience were spent getting to know the Lord and studying his word. God opened my eyes to scriptures that were not preached in the Christian world. Joseph Good had a program on the TBN network that was based on ancient Israel. With an understanding of our Hebrew roots, the Scriptures really came alive. God gave the Hebrew people a gauge to tell them about his plan for mankind. These feasts are called "Rehearsals or appointed times" in Hebrew *mo'ed*. The feasts are far too complex to discuss fully in this book, so we will only look at certain aspects as they apply to this study.

Even with an understanding of the Hebrew background, certain aspects of the feasts seem to be out of context: An example would be Matthew 27:15-26, where Barabbas was released from prison instead of Jesus. This picture of the scapegoat is one of the ceremonies from the Feast of Yom Kippur (the Day of Atonement). Jesus was crucified on Passover not on Yom Kippur, but was he really? I hope to show that Jesus did in fact fulfill Yom Kippur when he was on earth, under God's Time Frame not man's.

To understand God's Time Frame we need to go back to the beginning of time as we know it and work through to the current time. We can use what we know from God's plan to give us a border for future events. God's word is like a jigsaw puzzle as it pertains to Bible prophecy. This study will help establish a border of time around the major prophetic events in the Bible. You never really know how God is going fulfill prophecy. By using past events and God's *mo'ed* you can know the signs of the times.

Another question that kept on bothering me: How can we go and live with God forever and at the same time, have the Lord's reign last for only one thousand years? The answer has been right in front of us since the law was handed down on Mount Sinai. The Sabbath Day is the most important day in the Hebrew calendar. It is so important that it is listed as one of the Ten Commandments.

In order to study the feasts and festivals, we need to have a working knowledge of the lunar calendar and the layout of the Hebrew day. We also need to look at three, possibly four, levels of time to help us understand God's plan for the ages. This could explain the time frames in the first, second, and third heavens.

I pray this study will help in your understanding of God's plan and of future events, as your walk with the Lord Jesus Christ grows.

THE HEBREW CALENDAR

The Hebrew Day

Back to first grade. As a child we learned about telling time, the days of the week, and the months of the year. If you grew up with a Hebrew background, you already know these facts and can skip through this section rather quickly. If you were like me, your brain will be like scrambled eggs before you finally understand how the calendar works. I recommend that you spend some time in appendix C before you go any further. Look at how the two calendars compare; notice that the months don't line up. Our calendar is a solar calendar and the Hebrew calender is based on the moon. Look at the holidays for both calendars: our New Year is January 1; the Hebrew New Year is Tishri 1. This extra study will help your understanding. By the time you get to the chapter on the spring feasts, you will be able to grasp the concept better. Class is now in session!

Before we discuss the Hebrew calendar, there are several topics that need to be highlighted: the first of these topics is the layout of the Hebrew Day. Why is this unusual?

> **Genesis 1:3-5**
> *And God said, "Let there be light;" and there was light. God saw that the light was good, and separated the light from darkness. God called the light, "Day" and the darkness he called, "Night" and there was evening and there was morning, the first day.*

The Hebrew day starts at sundown and continues through to the next sundown. When working with the lunar calendar, this concept usually throws off our calculations. If we look at the charts below, we can see the difference in the days of the week between the Hebrew week and the solar week. The day changes at midnight on the solar day and at sundown on the Hebrew day. Morning and evening are both the same day on the solar day, but different days on the Hebrew calendar.

Solar Week

Morning	Sun.	Mon.	Tue.	Wed.	Thur.	Fri.	Sat.
Sundown	—	—	—	—	—	—	—
Evening	Sun.	Mon.	Tue.	Wed.	Thur.	Fri.	Sat.

Hebrew Week

Morning	Sun.	Mon.	Tues.	Wed.	Thur.	Fri.	Sat.
Sundown	—	—	—	—	—	—	—
Evening	Mon.	Tues.	Wed.	Thur.	Fri.	Sat.	Sun.

Temple Services

The daily temple services were held three times a day, with the first service in the evening.

> Psalms 55:17
> *Evening, morning and noon, I cry out in distress and, He hears my voice.*

These three daily services are still done in the synagogue today.

Hours of the Day

The next point that we need to cover is how the time of day was different at the time of Jesus than today. The hours of the day started at sunup and ended at sundown. The nighttime hours were not counted as part of the day. They were called watches. Watches will be covered later in the chapter.

> Luke 23:44
> *It was now about the sixth hour, and darkness came over the whole land until the ninth hour.*

The sixth hour would be noon, if sunrise were our equivalent of 6:00 A.M. The ninth hour would be our equivalent of 3:00 P.M..

7:00 A.M.	10:00 A.M.	Noon	3:00 P.M..
First Hr.	Fourth Hr.	Sixth Hr.	Ninth Hr.

Let's look at one more Scripture on the hours of the day.

> Matthew 20:5-6
> *So they went. He sent out again about the sixth hour and the ninth hour and did the same thing. About the eleventh hour, he went out and found still others standing around. He asked them, "Why have you been standing here all day long doing nothing?"*

The landowner went out at noon, 3:00 P.M. and 5:00 P.M. to hire workers for his vineyard.

WATCHES OF THE NIGHT

Sundials don't work at night. I can see it all now. Jesus is sitting by the campfire with his disciples. He says, "Hey Peter, take that lantern and go check the sundial." This is not very scriptural.

The nighttime hours in ancient Israel were divided up into three four-hour watches. The Israeli soldiers would keep watch for four hours at a time on the walls of the cities. This was to protect the inhabitants from invaders.

If sundown occurred at 6:00 P.M. the first watch of the night would be from 6:00 P.M. to 10:00 P.M. The middle watch would be from 10:00 P.M. until 2:00 A.M. The last watch is from 2:00 A.M. until 6:00 A.M.

> **Judges 7:19**
> *Gideon and the hundred men with him reached the edge of the camp at the beginning of the middle watch, just after they had changed the guard. They blew their trumpets and broke the jars that were in their hands.*

Our Scripture about Gideon says, "At the beginning of the middle watch." The time of Gideon's attack was between 10:00 P.M. and about 10:15 P.M.

> **I Samuel 11:11**
> *The next day Saul separated his men into three divisions; during the last watch of the night they broke into the camp of the Ammonites and slaughtered them until the heat of the day. Those who survived were scattered, so that no two of them were left together.*

As we move into New Testament times, we have another watch of the night that we need to be aware of. Roman watches were divided into four three-hour watches.

If sundown was 6:00 P.M., the first Roman watch would be 6:00 P.M. to 9:00 P.M.; the second watch, 9:00 P.M. until midnight; the third watch, midnight until 3:00 A.M.; and from 3:00 A.M. until 6:00 A.M. would be the fourth watch of the night.

In Matthew 14:25, Jesus would have walked on the water sometime between 3:00 A.M. and sunrise.

> Matthew 14:25
> *During the fourth watch of the night Jesus went out to them, walking on the lake.*

> Luke 12:38
> *It will be good for those servants whose master finds them ready, even if he comes in the second or third watch of the night.*

As we start to look at the feasts, the layout of the Hebrew day can provide almost exact times for events that occurred in the lives of many of the Old and New Testament personalities. These time frames can also be used to predict future events. We will look at some of these events in later chapters. Thank God that we have clocks that work at night.

The Hebrew Calendars

More than one calendar—you have got to be kidding! How do they keep track of all those months? I have a hard time remembering from one day to the next on one calendar. What will I do with more than one?

This is what I was thinking when I first found out that the Jewish people had more than one calendar. The part that I did not yet understand was that they used the same 12 months, but just had different starting points during the year. I feel better already. What would I have done if I had to learn the names of 48 months? I can tell you one thing—I wouldn't be writing this book.

The different calendars started on different days of the year. If the calendar started on April 15, one year later would be New Year's. But we would still have New Year's on January 1. This would be the New Year on the second calendar. April 15 could be the New Year for taxes. A bad example! Let's get some background on the calendar.

There are two major factors leading to the different types of calendars used on earth today: the sun and the moon. Let's look at what God said about the sun and the moon.

Genesis 1:14-16

And God said, "Let there be lights in the expanse of the sky to separate the day from the night, and let them serve as signs to mark seasons and days and years, and let them be lights in the expanse of the sky to give light on the earth." And it was so. God made two great lights—the greater light to govern the day and the lesser light to govern the night. He also made stars.

Egypt used a calendar similar to today's calendar, from morning to morning. The difference was that the month was still based on the moon. When the last quarter of the preceding moon disappeared, it was time for a new month. This worked out to a 30-day month and a 360-day year. Later under the New Year' section of this chapter, we can see this in the account of the flood that was given to Moses from God. Israel also used the 360-day year until Rome started the current calendar in A.D. 46.

Today we use 365 days, 5 hours, 48 minutes and 46 seconds as our year. This is the time of one rotation of the earth around our sun.

The lunar calendar is based on the rotation of the moon around the earth. A Hebrew month starts on the new moon. For the moon to make a complete rotation around the earth takes 29 days, 12 hours, and a little bit. A current lunar calendar year takes 354 days. A corrective month occurs seven times every 19 years, to catch up to the solar calendar. The calendar in appendix C is the 354- day calendar of today, not the one used in the Old Testament. Some of your calculations could be off by a day or so. This will be discussed more in depth later in the chapter.

THE MISHNAH

Now we jump from first grade to Bible college. Before we go any further, we need to introduce the Mishnah. The Mishnah is called "The Oral Torah" or Law: in Hebrew the word, *Torah* means "Law." When Moses was in God's presence on Mount Sinai, he received the Torah from God. The first five books of the Bible are the Law, Genesis through Deuteronomy.

The Mishnah is the practical application or instructions on how to perform God's laws. These instructions were passed down from Moses orally, and from father to son until, in 200 C.E., Rabbeinu, Hakadosh gathered the sages of his generation and compiled the oral teachings. The oldest known author of the Mishnah, next to God and Moses, is Ezra the prophet. A book in the Bible is named after him. Some of these names look like the ones I can't pronounce in the Bible.

The Mishnah is broken down into six major sections. These sections contain laws to govern Hebrew life.

1. Order of Seeds
2. Order of Festivals
3. Order of Women
4. Order of Civil Law
5. Order of Purity
6. Order of Cleanness

We will be looking at the second order, the Order of Festivals: in Hebrew, *mo'ed*, meaning "appointed times" or "rehearsals." This order contains the laws of how to perform the temple festivals, written about in the Torah or Law. Most of the temple services stopped when the temple was destroyed in A.D. 70. Some of the services were altered so that certain steps could be completed in the home. We will look at aspects of both types of services as they apply to this study.

As we begin to look at the feasts or *Seder Mo'ed*, we will begin to see God's plan for our redemption and salvation. *Seder Mo'ed* means "the order of appointed times."

Jesus fulfilled the spring feasts to the minute, while he was on earth, and we wait with anticipation for him to fulfill the fall feasts.

THE NEW YEAR'S

Football fans will love this: The Hebrew people have four New Year's Days. These days apply to the different aspects of society. Let's look at the Mishnah on this issue.

Rosh HaShanah 1:1

There are four New Year's Days:

1. On the First of Nisan is the New Year for Kings and for the Holidays.
2. On the First of Elul is the New Year for the Tithe of Animals.
3. On the First of Tishri is the New Year for the Years, for Sabbatical years, for the Jubilee Years, for the Planting of Trees, and for the Vegetables.
4. On the First of Shevat is the New Year for the Tree.

In this study we will look at only two of the Hebrew New Year's Days, the Civil and Religious. We will not cover the Tithe of Animals or the New Year for Planting Trees.

Back to second grade. Listed below is a layout of the months in the Hebrew calendars. The months are listed by number according to their order for the two Hebrew calendars. The names of the months are also listed along with the corresponding months of the Julian calendar. The month of Tishri is the first month of the civil calendar, and at the same time the seventh month on the religious calendar. Go back to appendix C and see how both calendars compare. This will help you to understand the later chapters.

Hebrew Calendar

Civil	Religious	Hebrew Month	Julian Month
1.	7.	Tishri or Ethanim	September - October
2.	8.	Cheshvan or Bul	October - November
3.	9.	Kislev	November - December
4.	10.	Tevet	December - January
5.	11.	Shevat	January - February
6.	12.	Adar	February - March
7.	1.	Nisan or Aviv	March - April
8.	2.	Iyar of Zif	April - May
9.	3.	Sivan	May - June
10.	4.	Tammuz	June - July
11.	5.	Av	July - August
12.	6.	Elul	August - September

A second month of Adar is added seven years out of every nineteen to bring the lunar calendar and solar calendar back into unity. Without the addition of this month, the 365-day solar calendar and the 354-day lunar calendar would become out of synchronization. The spring feasts would eventually take place in the fall on the lunar calendar. (Appendix C has an example of a current Hebrew calendar.)

The Civil Calendar

Time started on the civil calendar, not the religious calendar, which starts on the first of Nisan. How do we know this? The Mishnah says that the new year for counting the years starts on the first day of the month of Tishri. We could use our April 15 calendar that we talked about a few pages back as an example. Our years change on January 1, not on April 15, but it doesn't change the fact that taxes have to be paid by that date.

The second topic under this calendar is the earths' Sabbath. Every seventh year is to be a Sabbath of rest for the earth. No crops are to be planted for the entire year. The people are to live on the seeds that grow, without planting new ones. There are many laws to govern this situation. We will look at several of these laws in the next chapter.

There is one more event that is marked by this day (Tishri 1). The Year of Jubilee is an event that comes up every forty-nine years. This event really comes up every fifty years, because the first year after the forty-ninth year is zero. The Hebrew people have to live through a whole year to get to the first year after Jubilee. They don't go from forty-nine years to one year or they would lose a year. The years are counted after it is completed not before. Let's look at some Old Testament dates that have their basis in the civil calendar. When we look at the account of the flood, we can see the civil calendar.

> Genesis 7:11
> *In the six hundredth year of Noah's life, on the seventeenth day of the second month, on that day all the springs of the great deep burst forth and the floodgates of the heavens were opened.*

Using the civil calendar, the second month is the month of Cheshvan, or Bul. So the Flood started on the seventeenth of Bul.

> **Genesis 7:24**
> *The waters flooded the earth for a hundred and fifty days.*

Using the 30-day month, and counting ahead 150 days, on the civil calendar, we come to the month of Nisan or Aviv, the seventeenth day. 150days /30days = 5 months. The seventeenth of Aviv is the same day Jesus arose from the dead.

> **Genesis 8:3-4**
> *The water receded steadily from the earth. At the end of the hundred and fifty days the water had gone down, and on the seventeenth day of the seventh month the ark came to rest on the mountains of Ararat.*

The seventeenth of Aviv is the Feast of the Firstfruits of the Barley Harvest. Let's look at one more account of the Flood.

> **Genesis 8:13**
> *By the first day of the first month of Noah's six hundred and first year, the water had dried up from the earth.*

The first day of the first month is Tishri or Ethanim one. This is the New Year for the civil calendar, and the day of the Feast of Trumpets.

> **Genesis 8:14**
> *The twenty-seventh day of the second month the earth was completely dry.*

This statement puts the end of the Flood on the twenty-seventh of the month of Bul. There are no feasts on this day, but it is exactly 365 days from the start of the Flood. So God was using our current calendar, a solar calendar, so we could say the Flood lasted for one year.

God changed the Hebrew calendar from the civil to the religious in Exodus 12.

> **Exodus 12:2-3**
> *This month is to be for you the first month, the first month of your year. Tell the whole community of Israel that on the tenth day of this month each man is to take a lamb for his family, one for each household.*

The Hebrew family chooses a lamb on the tenth of Aviv for the Feast of Passover, which occurs on the fourteenth. We will look more at the feast of Passover in the chapter on the spring feasts.

The Religious Calendar

The religious calendar has its start on the first of the Hebrew month of Nisan. This is the start of the new year for kings. If a king comes to power any time during the past year, the second year of his reign is marked by the first of Nisan. So how do we use this?

For example, say that the king of England begins to reign in the month of December. When the first of January comes to pass, he would be in the second year of his reign, even though his reign is only two months long. This situation has an effect on all of the legal documents in the country. All legal documents such as the sale of property, wills, etc., are dated with the year of the current king's reign.

Most of the calendar references from Exodus 12 through the rest of the Bible are the religious calendar. The first day of the year is in the month of Nisan, not Tishri.

> **Exodus 16:1**
> *The whole Israelite community set out from Elim and came to the Desert of Sin, which is between Elim and Sinai, on the fifteenth day of the second month after they had come out of Egypt.*

If we look at our calendar chart, we see that the second month of the religious calendar is the month of Iyar.

Let's look at two Scriptures: one from the civil calendar and one from the religious that show the same calendar date, but different years. Remember the dates before Exodus 12 are in the civil calendar.

> **Genesis 8:13**
> *By the first day of the first month of Noah's six hundred and first year, the water had dried up from the earth.*

> **Nehemiah 7:73 and 8:1-2**
> *When the seventh month came and the Israelites had settled in their towns, all the people assembled as one man in the square before the Water Gate. They told Ezra the scribe to bring out the Book of the Law of Moses, which the Lord had commanded for Israel. So on the first day of the seventh month Ezra the priest brought the Law before the assembly, which was made up of men and women and all who were able to understand.*

If we look back at Nehemiah 8:1,2 and then Ezra 3:1, we see the same event taking place.

> **Ezra 3:1**
> *When the seventh month came and the Israelites had settled in their towns, the people assembled, as one man in Jerusalem.*

As you can see, the dates in the Bible seem to come together. The same dates are repeated over and over again. These are God's appointed times and rehearsals for those times. As we move into a study of the feasts, we will be able to see how perfectly Jesus fulfilled every aspect of the Law.

The fast days contain the same in-depth look at Jesus and the Jewish people as do the feasts. Zechariah tells us that the sad occasions for the fast days are no longer sad.

> **Zechariah 8:19**
> *This is what the LORD Almighty says: "The fasts of the fourth, fifth, seventh and tenth months will become joyful and glad*

occasions and happy festivals for Judah. Therefore, love truth and peace."

We will not be looking at the fast days, except for Yom Kippur, the Day of Atonement, in the seventh month of the Hebrew calendar. Yom Kippur is the holiest day of the year on the Hebrew calendar. This is a time when God judges the Israeli people for the past year and either forgives them or convicts them of their sins.

Before we move on, let's look at an example of the civil calendar being used after the religious calendar was started in Exodus 12.

> **Joel 2:23**
> *Be glad then, ye children of Zion, and rejoice in the LORD your God: for he hath given you the "former rain" moderately, and he will cause to come down for you the rain, the former rain, and the latter rain in the first month.*

In the first scripture, Zechariah 8:19, God is talking about the days of fasting in the months mentioned. These days will become joyous for the people of Judah.

In the second Scripture, "the latter rain" refers to the second coming of Christ and tells us this will happen in the first month.

The importance of God's appointed times can't be understated. A basic understanding of how the calendar works is a great help in studying what Jesus did while he was on earth. We can also apply these biblical dates to future events. When these dates are studied, you will see patterns develop to help with your Bible study.

THE SABBATH

THE MOST IMPORTANT DAY

The Sabbath is not on Sunday. The Jewish Sabbath starts on our Friday evening and runs through until the first three medium-sized stars can be seen in the sky on Saturday evening. Christians worship God on Sunday, the day Jesus was raised from the dead. The Sabbath is one of the most important days in the Bible. All the major feasts have underlying laws and regulations that come from it. If you can grasp the laws of the Sabbath, most of the feasts will be easier to understand. Let's look at Genesis 2:2-3.

> **Genesis 2:2-3**
> *By the seventh day God had finished the work he had been doing; so on the seventh day he rested from all his work. And God blessed the seventh day and made it holy, because on it he rested from all the work of creating that he had done.*

The Sabbath is the most important day in God's kingdom. It is the only one of the appointed times, or feast days, to be one of the Ten Commandments.

> **Exodus 20:8-11**
> *Remember the Sabbath day by keeping it holy. Six days you shall labor and do all your work, but the seventh day is a Sabbath, to the Lord your God. On it you shall not do any work, neither you, nor your son or daughter, nor your manservant or maidservant, nor your animals, nor the alien within your gates. For in six days the Lord made the heavens and the earth, the sea, and all that is in them, but he rested on the seventh day. Therefore the Lord blessed the Sabbath day and made it holy.*

Looking at Exodus 20:8-11, we see two requirements: The first to keep the day holy, with prayer and fellowship with God and one's family. The second requirement is that no labor should be done on this day. Let's look at what the Israeli people considered labor to be in the time of Moses. This will help us to understand how to keep the day holy. We will be able to see Jesus keeping some of these laws in the Scriptures.

Sabbath Laws

No "honey do's" on the Sabbath. This is the one law that needs to be added to the list of thirty-nine prohibited labors. I'll call this one number forty. I have watched many couples with fast-paced lifestyles during the work week come home and fight all weekend long. These couples add stress to their lives by forcing each other to complete projects and meet commitments at home. When they go back to work on Monday, they are worse off than they were on Friday.

The Sabbath forces us to slow down our lives and enjoy one another. The candle-lighting ceremony in the home just before sundown on Friday puts the stressful week behind us as we look forward to spending time with God and our families. The thirty-nine prohibited labors keep everyone from doing almost anything except spending time together and enjoying one another. Let's look at these laws.

The *mishkan* served as the tabernacle or tent of meeting during the forty years in the desert. This is the place where Moses would enter and meet with God.

Sages were Hebrew men of wisdom and high standing in the community. The sages deduced that the prohibited labors were the ones needed for the construction and maintenance of the tabernacle. The order of festivals under the Mishnah lists the thirty-nine prohibited labors.

Shabbos 7:2

The Thirty-Nine Prohibited Labors

1. Sowing
2. Plowing
3. Reaping
4. Gathering together
5. Threshing
6. Winnowing
7. Sorting
8. Grinding
9. Sifting
10. Kneading
11. Baking
12. Shearing wool
13. Whitening wool
14. Combing wool
15. Dyeing wool
16. Spinning
17. Mounting the warp
18. Setting two heddles
19. Weaving two threads
20. Removing two threads
21. Tying
22. Untying
23. Sewing two stitches
24. Tearing
25. Trapping a deer
26. Slaughtering a deer
27. Skinning a deer
28. Salting a deer
29. Tanning a deer
30. Smoothing a deer
31. Cutting a deer
32. Writing two letters
33. Erasing
34. Building
35. Demolishing
36. Extinguishing
37. Kindling
38. Striking the final blow
39. Transferring from domain to domain

Most of the forbidden labors have to do with sowing and weaving activities, along with construction and cooking. The Mishnah covers these laws in depth. Art Scroll Mishnah series *Shabbos* covers the items in detail with commentary.

Mounting the warp and setting the heddles (part of the weaving tool), two of the prohibited labors, have to do with weaving. One of the prohibited labors we might not understand is transferring from domain to domain.

Eruvin all

There are four domains

1. A private domain is an area at least four hand breathes square, marked by walls at least ten hand breathes high. It could even be a pit.
2. A public domain is city streets, highways, squares and roads at least sixteen cubits wide and must be frequented by many people.
3. An exempt area is an area less than 4 X 4 hand breathes, whose height is at least three hand breaths.
4. A *karmelis* is everything else.

The laws of transferring from domain to domain are set up to keep the Israeli population from carrying objects on the Sabbath. These laws help to keep the people from working on this Holy Day.

The laws of transferring from domain to domain allow some freedoms to carry objects if used properly. It could be possible to share a meal with the neighbors if a courtyard connects several homes. The enclosed area could be considered a public domain. To merge the courtyards, a loaf of bread is collected before the Sabbath, from each dwelling open to the courtyard, and placed in one dwelling for the duration of the Sabbath. The courtyard now becomes a private domain and people can carry items there.

The bread is a picture of Jesus. If we accept him, we can share the Sabbath with God and the others in the courtyard.

When Jesus was crucified, he had to be put in the tomb before the High Sabbath started. One of the reasons for this is the law of transferring from domain to domain. His body could not have been carried to the tomb by the Israeli people without breaking the law.

The laws on domains are part of the second tracate of the order of festivals under the Mishnah, called *Eruvin*. *Eruvin* helps establish rules for domain to domain transfers, as well as Sabbath boundaries.

The Sabbath boundary laws are also used to keep the Sabbath holy. A person is rabbinically prohibited from traveling on the Sabbath more than two thousand cubits from his place of dwelling. The place of dwelling is considered the place he found himself at the onset of the Sabbath. If a person was in a city, his place of dwelling is the entire city. He can walk two thousand cubits in any direction from the city.

It was possible to travel up to four thousand cubits, if the place you were to stop at for the Sabbath is two thousand cubits from your starting point. You could travel another two thousand cubits beyond your Sabbath location, as long as you would return before nightfall. So you could travel two thousand cubits in any direction from your Sabbath location.

There are more on the Laws of Erev in the Mishnah.

I believe the Laws of Erev were in effect in Luke 19 and Matthew 21.

> Luke 19:28-30
> *After Jesus had said this, he went on ahead, going up to Jerusalem. As he approached Bethphage and Bethany at the hill called The Mount of Olives, he sent two of his disciples, saying to them, "Go to the village ahead of you, and as you enter it, you will find a colt tied there, which no one has ever ridden. Untie it and bring it here:...*

> Matthew 21:17
> *And he left them and went out of the city to Bethany, where he spent the night.*

Both of these Scriptures are the same event. I believe the reason he went back to Bethany was the Laws of Erev. He could only travel two thousand cubits outside of Bethany before returning.

The Sabbath in the Home

We are going to take a very brief look at some of the ceremonies done in the home on the Sabbath. These are pictures of what the Sabbath in heaven will be like. The ceremonies are very involved so we will touch on some of the highlights. I recommend that you purchase a book on the Sabbath. There are too many steps to cover all the events of this day here.

Eighteen minutes before sundown, the Hebrew woman lights the Sabbath candles. Usually, at least two candles are lit. Many homes add one candle for each child. People that are single light their own candles, if no one is doing the lighting on their behalf.

A blessing is said over the candles. This is also a time to speak to God and express anything on your heart. Once the blessings are said, many go to the synagogue and return for the Sabbath meal.

The table is set with the finest china, crystal, silver or gold, and everyone is dressed to the utmost. The Sabbath is the special occasion and nothing is held back. There are many steps to the Sabbath meal. Through all the steps you can see God's hand and wonder what our Sabbath with God will be like.

Saturday morning everyone attends synagogue. After synagogue the second meal is served.

After the second meal, many take a Sabbath nap, study the Word of God, or socialize. The Sabbath Day can be the best day of the week for the kids—parents set up activities for the children. I wonder what our Heavenly Father has set up for us (His children) on the Sabbath. Can you see God down on the carpet playing games with us kids?

The third meal is a simple meal. It could be tea and bread. Psalm 23 is said at this meal, the last meal before the Havdalah ceremony.

The *Havadalah*, which means "to differentiate," is the ceremony that takes us from the Sabbath into the week that we are about to start. A braided candle is set aflame and fingers are held up to see the light and shadows dancing on them. The light and darkness symbolize wisdom and confusion, the hands are held before the light so we can see wisdom.

The Sabbath ends when the first three medium-sized stars in the sky are seen. The Sabbath is a time to slow down our lives and be filled with peace and joy. It makes you wonder—doesn't it?

The High Sabbaths

There are special days that are Sabbaths that are not on Saturday. These days are called High Sabbaths. Examples of these are Passover, the Feast of Trumpets, and the Day of Atonement, etc.... These feasts could fall on any day of the week and that day becomes a High Sabbath. On High Sabbath days all of the Sabbath laws must be followed, along with the laws for the given feast. This would be much like our holidays today—if Christmas falls on Tuesday, this day becomes a holiday.

For Jesus to arise on Sunday morning, he would have to have been crucified before Thursday night, Hebrew time. The Feast of Unleavened Bread would have started Thursday evening. This is a High Sabbath. Jesus would have been placed in the tomb Wednesday our time, before sundown, and arisen from the dead Sunday morning, fulfilling the following:

> Matthew 12:40
> *For as Jonah was three days and three nights in the belly of a huge fish, so the Son of Man will be three days and three nights in the Heart of the earth.*

> Mark 15:42
> *It was preparation day (that is, the day before the Sabbath). So as evening approached.*

Jesus would have been placed in the tomb before sundown because nothing was carried on the Sabbath.

> Matthew 28:1
> *After the Sabbath, at dawn on the first day of the week, Mary Magdalene and the other Mary went to look at the tomb.*

> Matthew 27:46
> *About the ninth hour Jesus cried out in a loud voice, "Eloi, Eloi, lama sabachthani!"—which means, "My God, my God, why have you forsaken me?"*

Looking at these four Scriptures, we can see that Jesus died between 3:00 and 3:30 in the afternoon on Wednesday our time, just before the start of the Passover. Sundown is the start of the new day. The feast of Unleavened Bread is a High Sabbath, so in this case the High Sabbath started on Thursday evening on the Hebrew calendar and Wednesday evening on our calendar, just after Jesus was put in the tomb.

There were two Sabbaths while Jesus was in the grave. The first Sabbath was for the feast of Unleavened Bread, which fell on Thursday during this year. The second Sabbath was the regular weekly Sabbath on Saturday.

The Earth's Sabbath

The earth also has a Sabbath every seven years. This event is marked by the civil calendar.

> Leviticus 25:2-5
> *Speak to the Israelites and say to them: "When you enter the land I am going to give you, the land itself must observe a Sabbath to the Lord. For six years sow your fields, and for six years prune your vineyards and gather their crops. But in the seventh year the land is to have a Sabbath of rest, a Sabbath to the Lord. Do not sow your fields or prune your vineyards. Do not reap what grows of itself or harvest the grapes of your untended vines. The land is to have a year of rest."*

> Deuteronomy 15:1-3
> *At the end of every seven years you must cancel debts. This is how it is to be done: Every creditor shall cancel the loan he has made to his fellow Israelite. He shall not require payment from his fellow Israelite or brother, because the Lord's time for canceling debts has been proclaimed. You may require payment from a foreigner, but you must cancel any debt your brother owes you.*

> Deuteronomy 15:9
> *Be careful not to harbor this wicked thought: The seventh year for canceling debts, is near, so that you do not show ill will toward your needy brother and give him nothing. He may appeal to the Lord against you, and you will be found guilty of sin.*

Think how different today's world would be if all debts were canceled every seven years. Our national debt wouldn't be a problem. My credit cards would be paid off!

One more major item happens on the seventh year; let's look at it:

> Deuteronomy 15:12-14
> *If a fellow Hebrew, a man or a woman, sells himself to you and serves you six years, in the seventh year you must let him go free. And when you release him, do not send him away Empty-handed. Supply him liberally from your flock, your threshing floor and your winepress. Give to him as the Lord your God has blessed you.*

There is one more topic under Sabbaths, the Year of Jubilee. Remember we are just touching some of the major points on these festivals or feasts. The Torah and Rabbinical writings are very detailed on these issues.

THE YEAR OF JUBILEE

The Year of Jubilee comes up every seven Sabbaths of years or forty-nine years and is marked by the civil calendar.

> Leviticus 25:8-11
> *Count off seven Sabbaths of years—seven times seven years—so that the seven Sabbaths of years amount to a period of forty-nine years. Then have the trumpet sounded everywhere on the tenth day of the seventh month; on the Day of Atonement sound the*

> *trumpet throughout your land. Consecrate the fiftieth year and proclaim liberty throughout the land to all its inhabitants. It shall be a jubilee for you; each one of you is to return to his family property and each to his own clan. The fiftieth year shall be a jubilee for you; do not sow and do not reap what grows of itself or harvest the untended vines.*

Remember that most calendar references after Exodus 12 are the civil calendar. The tenth day of the seventh month is Tishri 10, the Day of Atonement. This is the holiest day of the year, and the day that Sabbatical years are marked. The forty days leading up to the Day of Atonement are called "Elul," after the Hebrew month of Elul, and is a time of repentance. We will study more on the "time of Elul" later, under the fall feasts.

> **Leviticus 25:13**
> *In this Year of Jubilee everyone is to return to his own property.*

All the property reverts back to the original tribe and clan.

> **Leviticus 25:14-16**
> *If you sell land to one of your countrymen or buy any from him, do not take advantage of each other. You are to buy from your countryman on the basis of the number of years since the Jubilee. And he is to sell to you on the basis of the number of years left for harvesting crops. When the years are many, you are to increase the price, and when the years are few, you are to decrease the price, because what he is really selling you is the number of crops.*

In the above case, the property that was sold would revert back to the original owner at the time of Jubilee. The person who bought the property would return it to the original owner, at no cost.

There are many more laws in regard to the Sabbaths and the Year of Jubilee. There are many good references on these subjects. Please refer to them for a more in-depth study of these topics.

One Thousand Years Is as One Day

Let's get away from the feasts for a while and look at God's laws for heaven. The Hebrew people believe that the very Laws of Heaven were given to them when the Torah was given to Moses on Mount Sinai. These laws include all aspects of Israeli life, from the calendar, to weddings, feast days, using the rest room and on and on . . . All aspects of their lifestyle were given to them from God.

If we apply these laws to heaven and earth, secrets are revealed and Scripture begins to make more sense.

Time, in our plane, had not yet been created until the First Day was created, after the "Big bang." Let's look at Genesis:

> Genesis 1:5
> God called the light "day," and the darkness he called "night."
> And there was evening, and there was morning—the first
> day.

The very first day has to be the start of the New Year. Time has just started on this plane. The new year in Hebrew is called Rosh HaShanah or the Feast of Trumpets. This was the very first Feast of Trumpets in our universe.

Now we have a problem: God tells us that the length of days in heaven is not the same as on earth.

> 2 Peter 3:8
> But do not forget this one thing, dear friends: With the Lord a
> day is like a thousand years, and a thousand years are like a
> day.

> Psalms 90:4
> For a thousand years in your sight are like a day that has just
> gone by, or like a watch in the night.

So Peter and Moses (Psalm 90) are witnesses that one thousand years are as one day in God's sight.

Deuteronomy 19:15b
... A matter must be established by the testimony of two or three witnesses.

Deuteronomy 19:15b is brought up here to establish that the one thousand years are as one day. A second reference in the Bible to say that "one thousand years are as a watch in the night" could not be found. If a watch in the night were equal to one thousand years, "one day" would last six thousand years. A watch in the night for the Hebrew people is four hours long. Six four-hour watches would equal six thousand years.

The six thousand years could equal God's Time Frame, before the big bang, in Genesis 1:1-2, where the Spirit of God was hovering over the waters.

We will study "a day is as a thousand years" since we have two witnesses in this case.

When we look at the plane of God's Time Frame and man's plane intersecting, we could have the appearance of a wheel intersecting wheel as in Ezekiel. The Ezekiel 1:16 Scripture could be out of context here but the intersecting wheels create a picture of God's "former and latter rains."

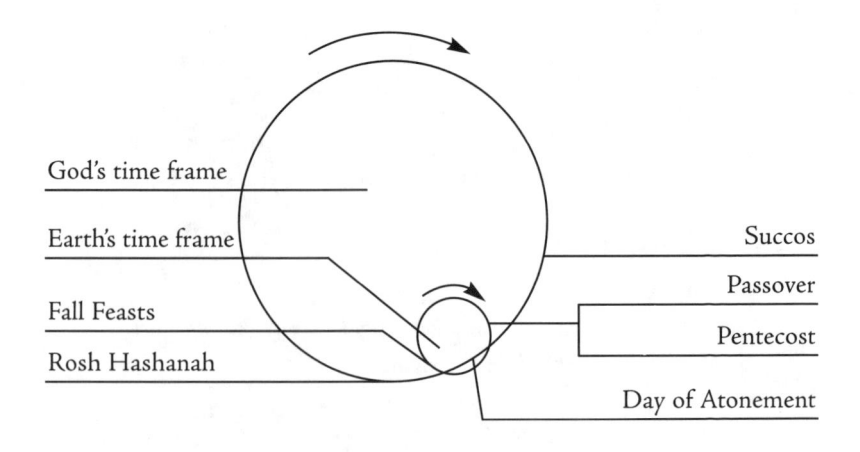

Ezekiel 1:16
This was the appearance and structure of the wheels: They sparkled like chrysolite, and all four looked alike. Each appeared to be made like a wheel intersecting a wheel.

You may ask, "Why draw the wheels this way?" (see the figure above). The large wheel is God's Time Frame, which equals 365 thousand years around the orbit. The small wheel is 365 days around our sun.

When time started with the Feast of Trumpets, both the earth and God's Time Frame had the same starting point, Rosh HaShanah (New Years). The difference between them is that one thousand years passed on earth's time frame before the first day ended on God's Time Frame.

Remember that the calendars are the same in heaven and on earth. The holidays and the Sabbaths are on the same dates on God's Time Frame as on earth. The difference is that in heaven they last for one thousand years. So the Day of Atonement on the tenth of the Hebrew month of Tishri, on earth's time frame, would also take place on the same date on God's Time Frame. Jesus was on earth during the Day of Atonement on the tenth of Tishri, on the "thousand years are as a day" calendar.

We are calling the second heaven "God's Time Frame" in this book; we know that God lives outside of this time frame, in the third heaven, or even a fourth time frame. We will look at this concept more in the last chapter.

As we continue, we will again run into feast days on God's Time Frame. On earth, we will have the feasts every year, as rehearsals for our next encounter. I know this is difficult to understand. We will look at this in more detail later in some of the following chapters.

Let's get back to diagram on the last page. Why do we have the two crossing points on the circles? This is to show the former and latter rains of Christ.

The former rain is believed to be the spring festivals and the latter rain is to be the fall festivals. Jesus fulfilled the spring festivals down to the minute according to Hebrew Law when he was on earth. Many are expecting the Lord Jesus to fulfill the fall festivals as well when he returns the next time.

What are the marks on the two circles? They are the location of the major feasts on the calendar if it were circular in nature. We don't really need two crossing points on the circles, but it just makes it easier to understand the concept of the former and latter rains of Christ.

The feasts have been fulfilled, time and time again, on man's time frame. These dates will continue to come up in the history of Israel until the end of the age.

Now we can see that both wheels work together, like gears. When man's feasts line up with God's, major events take place, like the creation of the universe and Jesus coming to earth. Some of the major coming events are the Wedding, the Sabbath, and the destruction of the earth by fire.

Another way to look at this concept is to look at a third or fourth grade math problem. Remember when we had to find the next two numbers in a sequence of numbers.

$$1, 2, 5, 6, 9 \ldots$$

In this case the next two numbers are 10 and 13. Let's look at a second set of numbers.

$$1, 4, 31, 25, 25$$

If we have our thinking caps on, we can see that these numbers are dates on the calendar. (January 1, July 4, October 31, November 25, and December 25). We could easily add several more dates of our own to this list. If we look at the Hebrew calendar for the first month, Tishri, and apply the previous concept about the holidays, it looks like this.

$$1, 7, 10, 12, 14, 15, 22$$

The first day is New Year's, the seventh is the Sabbath, the tenth is the Day of Atonement, the twelfth is the Wedding, the thirteenth the thousand-year reign of Christ, the fourteenth is the second Sabbath, the fifteenth is the first day of the Feast of Tabernacles and the twenty-second is the Eighth Day. (See appendix A)

If we multiply these days by one thousand years, we are looking at time in the second heaven, the major concept in this study. You will see later on that these dates line up and that the first three dates have been fulfilled. We are on the edge of fulfilling the fourth date, day twelve, the day of the Wedding. We will learn more about this one thousand years are as a day concept later; first we must learn about the feasts. The feasts will help us to confirm that the first three dates have been completed and give us a picture of future events from the Word of God.

THE SPRING FEASTS

Calendar, Calendar, Calendar… I know you are thinking, "When is he going to stop with this calendar thing?" If you have spent some time in appendix C, you probably have a headache. Something that you have taken for granted since grade school is very difficult to change, I know. It took me almost two years before I began to feel comfortable with all the new dates. Don't let this stop you from opening up the Word of God. The study of the Hebrew calendar helps us to unlock the Scriptures and leads us to many Bible truths. The reward is a much greater understanding of the Word of God.

We will be looking at the major feasts, of which there are four in the spring (the former rain) and three in the fall (the latter rain.) The purpose of this study is not only to learn about the feasts, but also to establish a border around God's puzzle, His time frame in the Bible.

Just like putting together a jigsaw puzzle, the feasts will help us to establish the proper time frames for God's prophecies. These are

Hebrew dates listed below. Passover and the Feast of Unleavened Bread are now considered one holiday. In Old Testament days they were separate holidays.

Spring Feasts

Name	Month & Day	Comments
Passover	Nisan 14	Remember Egyptian slavery. Pilgrimage feast.
Unleavened Bread	Nisan 15 - 21	Exodus from Egypt.
Firstfruits	The day after the Sabbath during Feast of Unleavened Bread.	Jesus rose from the dead. Ark of Noah came to rest.
Pentecost	50 days after Feast Firstfruits.	Moses received the law. Pilgrimage feast.

Pilgrimage Feasts

Before we go any farther, we need to say something about the pilgrimage feasts. Pilgrimage feasts are where everyone in Israel would travel to Jerusalem, to pay their tithes, pay their taxes, and worship at the temple. The three pilgrimage feasts are Passover, Pentecost, and the Feast of Tabernacles.

Two of the three pilgrimage feasts last for at least one week—Passover and the Feast of Tabernacles. The first and last days of these feasts are considered full holy days; the second through the sixth day of Passover and the second through the seventh day of Succos are considered ordinary holy days. Some of the prohibited labors of the Sabbath are allowed on these days. People cannot perform the full Sabbath laws for seven days or they could not function normally. Satan is destroyed on one of these days. We will look more at this in later chapters.

Passover and Unleavened Bread

We will look at both feasts together, because both occur only one day apart—Passover on Nisan 14, and Unleavened Bread on Nisan 15-21. Preparations for both of these feasts are going on at the same time.

Let's look at the last week of Jesus' earthly ministry. We will lay out the last week of his ministry on earth by looking at the holidays and activities that he fulfilled. The week we are showing below looks slightly different from the one in appendix C. I hope this will help you throughout this section. Remember, the date changes in the evening.

Month		Sun.	Mon.	Tues.	Wed.	Thur.	Fri.	Sat.	Sun.
Nisan	Morning	10	11	12	13	14	15	16	17
	Evening	11	12	13	14	15	16	17	18

On the tenth of Nisan the Passover lamb is chosen. Jesus eats the last supper with the disciples on the evening of the fourteenth, and is killed later in the same day. This is Passover. He must be placed in the ground before the feast of Unleavened Bread starts on the evening of the fifteenth because it is a High Sabbath. The regular weekly Sabbath starts on the sixteenth.. Jesus is raised from the dead on the seventeenth, the Feast of Firstfruits. This is just a quick look at Holy Week; we will study these items more in depth later in the chapter.

When we look at the New Testament, we need to be able to separate the ceremonies of both Passover and Unleavened Bread. This way we will be able to see how Jesus fulfilled both feasts.

The Passover

We all know the story of the exodus from Egypt. The Hebrew people were to slay a lamb on the fourteenth of Nisan and put its blood on the doorposts of their homes. God was going to pass through the land that night and kill all the firstborn men and animals and destroy all of the Egyptian gods. The house that had the lamb's blood on the doorposts would be safe from the plague of death. The blood of the lamb is a picture of the blood of Christ, which protects us from the Devil and the plagues of today. Let's study the feast.

> **Numbers 9:2-3**
> *Have the Israelites celebrate the Passover at the appointed time. Celebrate it at the appointed time, at twilight on the fourteenth day of this month, in accordance with all its rules and regulations.*

On the tenth day of the first month of Nisan, or Aviv, each man is to take a lamb for his family or household. They must take care of the lamb until the fourteenth day of Nisan, when all of the community of Israel must slaughter it at twilight. Twilight is just before sundown on the fourteenth of Nisan. Remember that the day starts in the evening. After the sun goes down, the fifteenth day of Nisan would start. During these four days the lamb is inspected—not a spot or wrinkle can be found or the sacrifice is invalid, and another lamb must be chosen.

The following Scripture is the Passover lamb coming to the temple, to be inspected by the people.

> **Matthew 21:1-11**
> *As they approached Jerusalem and came to Bethphage on the Mount of Olives, Jesus sent two disciples, saying to them, "Go to the village ahead of you, and at once you will find a donkey tied there, with her colt by her. Untie them and bring them to me. If anyone says anything to you, tell him that the Lord needs them, and he will send them right away." This took place to fulfill what was spoken through the prophet: "Say to the Daughter of Zion, 'See, your king comes to you, gentle and riding on a donkey, on a colt, the foal of a donkey.'"*
>
> *The disciples went and did as Jesus had instructed them. They brought the donkey and the colt, placed their cloaks on them, and Jesus sat on them. A very large crowd spread their cloaks on the road, while others cut branches from the trees and spread them on the road. The crowds that went ahead of him and those that followed shouted, "Hosanna to the Son of*

David!" "Blessed is he who comes in the name of the Lord!" "Hosanna in the highest!"

When Jesus entered Jerusalem, the whole city was stirred and asked, "Who is this?" The crowds answered, "This is Jesus, the prophet from Nazareth in Galilee."

The Pharisees and Sadducees ask Jesus many questions, to search for spot or wrinkle, but none can be found.

Matthew 22:41
While the Pharisees were gathered together, Jesus asked them, Saying, What think ye of Christ? Whose son is he? They say unto him, The son of David. He saith unto them, How then doth David in spirit call him Lord, saying, The Lord said unto my Lord, Sit thou on my right hand, till I make thine enemies thy footstool? If David then call him Lord, how is he his son? And no man was able to answer him a word, neither durst any man from that day forth ask him any more questions.

The evening of Passover, the day before the lamb is to be slain, preparations for the Feast of Unleavened Bread are to begin.

Exodus 12:12-17
For I will pass through the land of Egypt this night, and will smite all the firstborn in the land of Egypt, both man and beast; and against all the gods of Egypt I will execute judgment: I am the LORD. And the blood shall be to you for a token upon the houses where ye are: and when I see the blood, I will pass over you, and the plague shall not be upon you to destroy you, when I smite the land of Egypt.

And this day shall be unto you for a memorial; and ye shall keep it a feast to the LORD throughout your generations; ye shall keep it a feast by an ordinance for ever. Seven days shall ye eat Unleavened Bread; even the first day ye shall put away leaven out of your houses: for whosoever eateth leavened bread from the first day until the seventh day, that soul shall be cut off from Israel. And in the first day there shall be an holy convocation, and in the seventh day there shall be a holy convocation to you; no manner of work shall be done in them, save that which every man must eat, that only may be done of you.

And ye shall observe the feast of Unleavened Bread; for in this selfsame day have I brought your armies out of the land of Egypt: therefore shall ye observe this day in your generations by an ordinance for ever.

Just before sundown near the end of the fourteenth day, the Passover Lamb is slain. At the time the children of Israel were in Egypt, the blood of the lamb on the doorposts covered Israel's dwellings and protected them against the destructive plague that killed all the firstborn of Egypt. Let's see what the Mishnah has to say about the Passover sacrifice.

> Pesachim 5:1
>
> *The (afternoon) daily offering is (usually) slaughtered at eight and a half (hours).*
>
> *On the eve of pesach it is slaughtered at seven and a half (hours) and offered at eight and a half (hours) whether it is a weekday or the Sabbath.*
>
> *If the eve of pesach fell on the eve of the Sabbath, it is slaughtered at six and a half (hours), and offered at seven and a half (hours). The pesach (sacrifice) is offered after it.*

So Jesus, our Passover sacrifice, was offered up after the daily sacrifice.

> Matthew 27:46a
> *About the ninth hour Jesus cried out in a loud voice... .*

The ninth hour is 3:00 P.M.

> Matthew 27:50
> *And when Jesus had cried out again in a loud voice, he gave up his spirit.*

Jesus died between 3:00 and 3:30 P.M.

> Pesachim 7:1a
> How do we roast the Pesach? We bring a spit of pomegranate wood
> and thrust it (through) from its mouth to its anus and place its knees
> and its entrails inside it (these are) the words of R' Yose HaGlili

Jesus was a picture of this sacrifice—he was hung on a cross. The lamb was to be cooked while standing straight up on the stake, not lying down in the pan. The blood of the Passover sacrifice is to be collected beneath the lamb, to be offered up to God.

The entrails wrapped around the lamb are a picture of the Roman spear in his side.

> John 14:33-34
> But when they came to Jesus and found that he was already dead,
> they did not break his legs. Instead, one of the soldiers pierced
> Jesus' side with a spear, bringing a sudden flow of blood and water.

The Father will sacrifice the Passover offering for the first one who reaches Jerusalem. What does the Mishnah say about this?

> Pesachim 8:3
> "If one says to his, sons' I will slaughter the Passover offering for
> the first among you to reach Jerusalem."
> "As soon as he arrives in Jerusalem, he has acquired his portion,
> and he acquired his brother's portion for them."
> "The first brother can divide up the portions any way he wants,
> because he was the first to arrive."

> Pesachim 8:4
> "You must be registered for your portion of the Passover lamb."

So how can you be registered for your portion? ...By accepting Jesus as our Lord and Savior, the Lord will give us our portions. Jesus is the firstfruit, the first son to reach The New Jerusalem.

The Feast of Unleavened Bread

Which feast is it? This can get a little complicated—Passover is on the fourteenth of Nisan and the Feast of Unleavened Bread starts on the fifteenth of Nisan. During Passover, ceremonies are also being completed for the Feast of Unleavened Bread. The search for leaven in the home on Passover is actually a custom for the Feast of Unleavened Bread. The search for leaven has to be completed before the start of the feast on the fifteenth. The Passover lamb is slain late in the day just before sundown, and is eaten in the evening during the start of the Feast of Unleavened Bread. Yada Yada Yada...I know that all of you understand this, but just incase you don't, let's look at the Passover Haggadah.

The Haggadah

Haggadah means descriptions of historical events, legends and proverbs.

These are the customs of the Hebrew people for Passover. The search for leaven occurs on Passover, but the customs are preparation for the Feast of Unleavened Bread.

In the evening on the fourteenth of Nisan (Passover) the lights are turned off and the father leads his family in a search for hidden leaven.

Ten small pieces of bread were hidden throughout the house by the mother on the day before Passover. A candle, a feather, a wooden spoon, and a cloth or paper sack is used in the search. As each piece of leaven is found, the feather is used to sweep it into the wooden spoon. After all the leaven is found, the feather, the bread, and the spoon are wrapped in the cloth and cast out the door as the father says this blessing:

All leaven and leavened things that are in my possession of which I have neither seen, nor removed, and of which I know nothing about, shall be nullified and considered public like the dust of the earth.

The following morning, the father picks up the cloth containing *chametz*, the wooden spoon and the feather, and goes to the synagogue where a fire is built. As he throws his bundle into the fire, he recites a blessing and declares that his house is now free of leaven and prepared for the Feast of Unleavened Bread.

> I Corinthians 5:6-8
> *Your boasting is not good. Don't you know that a little yeast works through the whole batch of dough? Get rid of the old yeast that you may be a new batch without yeast—as you really are. For Christ, our Passover lamb, has been sacrificed. Therefore let us keep the Festival, not with the old yeast, the yeast of malice and wickedness, but with bread without yeast, the bread of sincerity and truth.*

> Zephaniah 1:12
> *At that time I will search Jerusalem with lamps and punish those who are complacent, who are like wine left on its dregs, who think, "The LORD will do nothing, either good or bad."*

The leaven is symbolic of sin. Sin (leaven) is searched out by using the candle, a picture of God's light exposing the sin. The Holy Spirit, symbolic of the feather, is used to judge the sin.

> Romans 6:23
> *For the wages of sin is death, but the gift of God is eternal life in Christ Jesus our Lord.*

> 2 Corinthians 5:21
> *God made him who had no sin to be sin for us, so that in him we might become the righteousness of God.*

We have already looked at some of the preparations and customs for the Feast of Unleavened Bread.

As we read through the Mishnah, Pesachim 1:1-4; *chametz* means leaven.

> Pesachim 1:1-2
> *The evening of the fourteenth (of Nisan) we must search for the "chametz" by the light of a candle. Any place into which "chametz" is not brought, does not require a search.*
> *So why have the Sages said, "Two rows of a (wine) cellar (must be searched)? A place into which we bring "chametz." Beis*

Shammai say: "Two rows over the entire front of the (wine) cellar (must be searched). But Beis Hillel say: "The two outer rows which are the uppermost."

We need not be concerned that a weasel may have dragged (chametz) from house to house, or from place to place. For if so (then let us be concerned) from courtyard to courtyard and from town to town. There is; (then) no end to the matter.

Matthew 26:57-58
Those who had arrested Jesus took him to Caiaphas, the high priest, where the teachers of the law and the elders had assembled. But Peter followed him at a distance, right up to the courtyard of the high priest ...

Jesus went from courtyard to courtyard just like the Mishnah says. The angry mob was still looking for leaven in Jesus. They were still checking him by candlelight to see if he was a perfect sacrifice.

Matthew 27:2
They bound him, led him away and handed him over to Pilate, the governor.

Jews were not allowed in Roman homes so I believe Jesus was in Pilate's wine cellar. Back to the Mishnah, PESACHIM 1:1 "The weasel was still looking for leaven." Jesus was beaten. They did anything to get him to sin.

Luke 23:6-7
On hearing this, Pilate asked if the man was a Galilean. When he learned that Jesus was under Herod's jurisdiction, he sent him to Herod, who was also in Jerusalem at that time.

Luke 23:11
Then Herod and his soldiers ridiculed and mocked him. Dressing him in an elegant robe, they sent him back to Pilate.

Then Jesus went from town to town.

> Pesachim 1:3-4
> R' Yehudah says: We must search on the evening of the fourteenth, or on the morning of the the fourteenth, or at the time of removal.
>   But the Sages say: If one did not search on the evening of the fourteenth, he must search on the (day of the) fourteenth; if he did not search on the (day of the) fourteenth, he must search during the festival; if he did not search during the festival, he must search after the festival. That which he leaves over, he should place in hiding, so that it will not be necessary to search for it (again).
>   R' Meir says: We may eat (chametz) the entire fifth (hour), and we must burn (it) at the onset of the sixth (hour).
>   R' Yehudah also said: We may eat (chametz) the entire fourth (hour), but we suspend (it) the entire fifth (hour), and we must burn it at the onset of the sixth (hour).

The soldiers looked for leaven in Jesus all night long, even when he was on the cross.

> Luke 23:44
> It was now about the sixth hour, and darkness came over the whole land until the ninth hour.

At the sixth hour, the time the Mishnah says the leaven is to be burned, darkness came over the whole land.

> Luke 23:50-54
> Now there was a man named Joseph, a member of the Council, a good and upright man, who had not consented to their decision and action. He came from the Judean town of Arimathea and he was waiting for the kingdom of God. Going to Pilate, he asked for Jesus' body. Then he took it down, wrapped it in linen cloth and placed it in a tomb cut in the rock, one in which no one had yet been laid. It was Preparation Day, and the Sabbath was about to begin.

The Lord had to be put in the ground before the High Sabbath started, the first day of the Feast of Unleavened Bread.

With Jesus being placed in the grave most of the activities on Nisan 14 are now complete. The Lamb that was sacrificed is now eaten. Due to the special case of Jesus being here on earth at this time, there are still some things that need to be covered. These things occur on the fourteenth of Nisan. We will look at these during the fall feasts.

The purpose of the first evening of the Feast of Unleavened Bread is to remember as much about the Exodus from Egypt as possible. This is one of the steps in the Seder service. The service is to commemorate the story of Israel being set free from the bondage of Egypt.

The Seder service is a fifteen-step service that is very detailed, much too detailed to cover fully here. We will take a quick look at some of the steps in the service. Hatikva Ministries has an excellent book on this subject.

> Exodus 13:8
> *On that day tell your son, "I do this because of what the LORD did for me when I came out of Egypt."*

Starting at the age of six, it was the father's job to teach his son the Torah.

The Four Symbols

There are four symbols used during the Seder service. These items are to help remind the Jewish people of their deliverance from Egypt and the mighty hand of God who brought them out.

The first symbol is the roasted shank bone, called *ceroah*, Hebrew for "arm."

> Exodus 12:3-9
> *Tell the whole community of Israel that on the tenth day of this month each man is to take a lamb for his family, one for each household. If any household is too small for a whole lamb, they must share one with their nearest neighbor, having*

taken into account the number of people there are. You are to determine the amount of lamb needed in accordance with what each person will eat. The animals you choose must be year-old males without defect, and you may take them from the sheep or the goats. Take care of them until the fourteenth day of the month, when all the people of the community of Israel must slaughter them at twilight. Then they are to take some of the blood and put it on the sides and tops of the doorframes of the houses where they eat the lambs. That same night they are to eat the meat roasted over the fire, along with bitter herbs, and bread made without yeast. Do not eat the meat raw or cooked in water, but roast it over the fire—head, legs and inner parts.

When God saw the blood of sacrifice, He passed over the houses of the Israeli people.

I Corinthians 5:7b
...For Christ, our Passover lamb, has been sacrificed.

Isaiah 53:1
Who has believed our message and to whom has the arm of the LORD been revealed?

The next symbol is the three *matzot* showing the Unleavened Bread. During the Seder, the middle *matzah* or Unleavened Bread, is broken, wrapped in linen, and hidden. The children then go throughout the house to find the broken piece of *matzah*. The child who finds it redeems it from the father of the house for money.

Jesus took the middle piece of *matzah*, broke it and said:

I Corinthians 11:24b
This is my body, which is for you; do this in remembrance of me.

The *matzah* is striped, pierced, and without leaven.

Matthew 27:26
Then he released Barabbas to them. But he had Jesus flogged, and handed him over to be crucified.

Psalms 22:16
Dogs have surrounded me; a band of evil men has encircled me, they have pierced my hands and my feet.

Isaiah 53:5b
… and by his wounds we are healed.

Isaiah 53:9
He was assigned a grave with the wicked, and with the rich in his death, though he had done no violence, nor was any deceit in his mouth.

The third symbol is the roasted egg. This reminds the Hebrew people of the loss of the temple where sacrifices were offered up.

Charoset is a mixture of apples, spices, nuts, and grapes. It represents the mortar used while building Egyptian cities.

Parsley is like the hyssop branch used in the first Passover service.

The fruit of the vine is drunk, as a symbol of joy and thanksgiving. Four cups of wine are consumed during this service and they represent the promises in the following passage:

Exodus 6:6-7
Therefore, say to the Israelites: "I am the Lord, and I will bring you out from under the yoke of the Egyptians. I will free you from being slaves to them, and I will redeem you with an outstretched arm and with mighty acts of judgment. I will take you as my own people, and I will be your God. Then you will know that I am the Lord your God, who brought you out from under the yoke of the Egyptians."

So how does the study of the Feast of Unleavened Bread pertain to us today? Just as Israel was delivered from the Egyptians and Pharaoh by the power of God, Jesus was delivered from death and Satan's wrath. He was the first to reach the New Jerusalem—now it is up to us.

The Feast of Firstfruits

Which fruit is first? It has to be an orange, maybe an apple. No, it has to be a peach. This is what I was thinking when I heard the title of this feast for the first time. Later I learned that this feast had nothing to do with fruit, but that it was offering time for the barley harvest. The tithes on the first ripe barley grain were brought to the temple and given to the priests. This barley was used in temple services, as well as food for the priests. The first portion of everything God gives to us belongs to Him. Jesus is the first Son of God and the first Son of God to enter the New Jerusalem. He is the firstfruit.

The Festival of Firstfruits falls during the week of the Feast of Unleavened Bread. The day after the weekly Sabbath, the first Sunday after the fifteenth of Nisan, is the Feast of Firstfruits.

> **Leviticus 23:9-11a**
> The LORD said to Moses, "Speak to the Israelites and say to them: 'When you enter the land I am going to give you and you reap its harvest, bring to the priest a sheaf of the first grain you harvest. He is to wave the sheaf before the LORD so it will be accepted on your behalf;…'"

This is the same day that Israel crossed through the Red Sea. The death of Pharaoh ended his rights of ownership over the children of Israel. Pharaoh is a picture of Satan's hold on our lives.

> **Exodus 14:13-31**
> Moses answered the people, "Do not be afraid. Stand firm and you will see the deliverance the LORD will bring you today. The Egyptians you see today you will never see again. The LORD will fight for you; you need only to be still." Then the LORD said to Moses, "Why are you crying out to me? Tell the Israelites to move on. Raise your staff and stretch out your hand over the

sea to divide the water so that the Israelites can go through the sea on dry ground. I will harden the hearts of the Egyptians so that they will go in after them. And I will gain glory through Pharaoh and all his army, through his chariots and his horsemen. The Egyptians will know that I am the LORD when I gain glory through Pharaoh, his chariots and his horsemen."

Then the angel of God, who had been traveling in front of Israel's army, withdrew and went behind them. The pillar of cloud also moved from in front and stood behind them, coming between the armies of Egypt and Israel. Throughout the night the cloud brought darkness to the one side and light to the other side; so neither went near the other all night long. Then Moses stretched out his hand over the sea, and all that night the LORD drove the sea back with a strong east wind and turned it into dry land. The waters were divided, and the Israelites went through the sea on dry ground, with a wall of water on their right and on their left.

The Egyptians pursued them, and all Pharaoh's horses and chariots and horsemen followed them into the sea. During the last watch of the night the LORD looked down from the pillar of fire and cloud at the Egyptian army and threw it into confusion. He made the wheels of their chariots come off so that they had difficulty driving. And the Egyptians said, "Let's get away from the Israelites! The LORD is fighting for them against Egypt."

Then the LORD said to Moses, "Stretch out your hand over the sea so that the waters may flow back over the Egyptians and their chariots and horsemen." Moses stretched out his hand over the sea, and at daybreak the sea went back to its place. The Egyptians were fleeing toward it, and the LORD swept them into the sea. The water flowed back and covered the chariots and horsemen—the entire army of Pharaoh that had followed the Israelites into the sea. Not one of them survived.

But the Israelites went through the sea on dry ground, with a wall of water on their right and on their left. That day the LORD saved Israel from the hands of the Egyptians, and Israel saw the Egyptians lying dead on the shore. And when the

> Israelites saw the great power the LORD displayed against the
> Egyptians, the people feared the LORD and put their trust in
> him and in Moses his servant.

There are several major happenings on the first day of the Feast of Firstfruits.

We have already looked at Noah and the flood and how God delivered him and his family. The seventeenth day of the seventh month, is the seventeenth of Nisan, on the civil calendar.

> **Genesis 8:3-4**
> *The water receded steadily from the earth. At the end of the hundred and fifty days the water had gone down, and on the seventeenth day of the seventh month, the ark came to rest on the mountains of Ararat.*

There is at least one more major happening on this feast day. Jesus rose from the dead.

> **Luke 24:1-3**
> *On the first day of the week, very early in the morning, the women took the spices they had prepared and went to the tomb. They found the stone rolled away from the tomb, but when they entered, they did not find the body of the Lord Jesus.*

THE FEAST OF PENTECOST

What does *Pentecost* mean? The original meaning is fifty days from the feast of Unleavened Bread. So what does this mean to you if you are Pentecostal? The Jewish people were given this day as a feast day from the Lord. Moses received that first set of tablets from God on this day, the ones he later broke when he saw the sin of the people. Later the disciples were filled with the power of the Holy Spirit on this day. I hope *Pentecostal* means "filled with the power of the spirit" and not "fifty days from the Feast of Unleavened Bread." My dictionary has twelve hundred pages and there is not a definition for Pentecostal in there anywhere. Don't write me bad letters—it's true. Let's look at a festival where many Christians have taken the name *Pentecost* as their own.

The children of Israel left Egypt on the fifteenth of Nisan or Aviv and traveled in the desert for forty-seven days until they reached Mount Sinai. There they purified themselves for three days and approached Mount Sinai. Fifty days after the Feast of Firstfruits, is the Feast of Weeks, or Pentecost. Many important things happened on this day as well.

> Leviticus 23:15-21
> *"From the day after the Sabbath, the day you brought the sheaf of the wave offering, count off seven full weeks. Count off fifty days up to the day after the seventh Sabbath, and then present an offering of new grain to the LORD. From wherever you live, bring two loaves made of two-tenths of an ephah of fine flour, baked with yeast, as a wave offering of First fruits to the LORD. Present with this bread seven male lambs, each a year old and without defect, one young bull and two rams. They will be a burnt offering to the LORD, together with their grain offerings and drink offerings—an offering made by fire, an aroma pleasing to the LORD. Then sacrifice one male goat for a sin offering and two lambs, each a year old, for a fellowship offering. The priest is to wave the two lambs before the LORD as a wave offering, together with the bread of the Firstfruits. They are a sacred offering to the LORD for the priest. On that same day you are to proclaim a sacred assembly and do no regular work. This is to be a lasting ordinance for the generations to come, wherever you live."*

So what happened at Mount Sinai?

> Exodus Rabbah 5:9
> *When God gave the Torah on Sinai, He displayed untold marvels to Israel with his voice. God spoke and the voice reverberated throughout the world; all the people witnessed the thundering.*

> God's voice was split up into seventy voices, in seventy languages, so that all the nations could understand.

The Midrash says:

> On the occasion of giving of the Torah, the Children of Israel not only, heard the Redeemer voice, but actually saw the sound waves as they emerged from the Redeemer's mouth. They visualized them as a fiery substance.
>
> Each commandment that left HaShem's mouth traveled around the camp and came back to every Jew individually asking him if he accepts the commandment. Finally, after everyone answered 'Yes,' the fiery substance engraved its self on the tablets. This is the first set of tablets that Moses brought down the mountain. These tablets were broken by Moses when he saw Israel's sin.

Let's look at what Jesus says about the Feast of Weeks:

Luke 24:45-49
Then he opened their minds so they could understand the Scriptures. He told them, "This is what is written: The Christ will suffer and rise from the dead on the third day, and repentance and forgiveness of sins will be preached in his name to all nations, beginning at Jerusalem. You are witnesses of these things. I am going to send you what my Father has promised; but stay in the city until you have been clothed with power from on high.

Acts 1:4-5
On one occasion, while he was eating with them, he gave them this command: "Do not leave Jerusalem, but wait for the gift my Father promised, which you have heard me speak about. For John baptized with water, but in a few days you will be baptized with the Holy Spirit.

Acts 2:1-13

When the day of Pentecost came, they were all together in one place. Suddenly a sound like the blowing of a violent wind came from heaven and filled the whole house where they were sitting. They saw what seemed to be tongues of fire that separated and came to rest on each of them. All of them were filled with the Holy Spirit and began to speak in other tongues as the Spirit enabled them.

Now there were staying in Jerusalem God-fearing Jews from every nation under heaven. When they heard this sound, a crowd came together in bewilderment, because each one heard them speaking in his own language. Utterly amazed, they asked: "Are not all these men who are speaking Galileans? Then how is it that each of us hears them in his own native language? Parthians, Medes and Elamites; residents of Mesopotamia, Judea and Cappadocia, Pontus and Asia, Phrygia and Pamphylia, Egypt and the parts of Libya near Cyrene; visitors from Rome (both Jews and converts to Judaism); Cretans and Arabs—we hear them declaring the wonders of God in our own tongues!" Amazed and perplexed, they asked one another, "What does this mean?"

Some, however, made fun of them and said, "They have had too much wine."

We see in Acts almost the same experience that Israel had at Mount Sinai. God's voice was divided up into seventy languages, so every nation could understand.

The book of Ruth takes place during the Feast of Firstfruits and ends at the Feast of Pentecost. Ruth is redeemed on Pentecost. She also becomes a bride, a picture of the Church becoming the Bride of Christ.

The first night of Pentecost, all Israel stays awake studying the Law. The *Midrash* says, "Before Israel received the Torah, the whole camp of Israel overslept. God appeared amid thunder and lightening and Moses had to rouse them from their sleep. By staying awake all night, the people will not make the same mistake."

Pentecost is the second Pilgrimage festival of the year. The firstfruits of the wheat harvest are brought to Jerusalem on this day, along with the tithes.

> Acts 20:16
> *Paul had decided to sail past Ephesus to avoid spending time in the province of Asia, for he was in a hurry to reach Jerusalem, if possible, by the day of Pentecost.*

It is customary to eat dairy foods on Pentecost, because God had just given the nation of Israel the Dietary Laws. Milk is given to children and Israel was a new child or nation.

This concludes the spring festivals, or the former rain, showing the Lord's first coming. The spring festivals were all fulfilled to the day and hour and teach God's principles.

Due to the time of Jesus' arrival on earth, there is one more feast than normal at this time. God's Time Frame intervenes and a feast is added to the normal spring feasts, the Day of Atonement.

THE DAY OF ATONEMENT?

Yom Kippur, one of the feasts that normally arrives in the fall on man's time frame, is at hand on God's Time Frame among the spring feasts. This happening is out of context with the normally accepted theories. Under these theories, the spring feasts are all grouped together into what is called the former rain, to be fulfilled during the first coming of the Lord. The fall feasts are grouped together into the latter rain and will be fulfilled when the Lord returns in the fall season. Not only was Jesus the Passover sacrifice, but he was also our High Priest. This is how he could atone for our sins with his own blood.

The Day of Atonement (Yom Kippur) is on the "one thousand years as one day" calendar at the same time as Passover, Unleavened Bread, and Firstfruits. We will look at the Day of Atonement, along with the fall feasts and we will be able to see how Jesus fulfilled this feast, in the spring while he was on earth.

We already looked at Jesus fulfilling the spring feasts to the letter of the law. As we move into the fall feasts, we will be able to see how he kept the Day of Atonement.

Appendix A shows how God's Time Frame fits into Earth's Time Frame.

The fall feasts, or latter rain, of Jesus must be fulfilled on earth's time frame. The Feast of Trumpets and the Day of Atonement have already been fulfilled on God's Time Frame. The next major feast on God's Time Frame is the Feast of Tabernacles.

THE FALL FEASTS

On September 11, the World Trade Center was destroyed. So what does this terrible event have to do with the Jewish Feasts and Festivals? As we said before the feasts are called *mo'ed*, which can be translated "rehearsals or appointed times." There is a forty-day season of repentance that starts with the first day of the month of Elul and ends with the feast of Yom Kippur. The whole world came together to mourn the loss of loved ones and to seek God for guidance and forgiveness. God did not create this situation—He loves us more than we can understand, and He will turn this around for good. September 11 translates to the 22 of Elul. This date is about halfway through the time of repentance.

I have seen this time of Elul come alive for me for several years now. If I have a problem with someone or a given situation over the last year, where I am harboring anger toward someone, God always deals with me during this time of year. You have to be able to put the situation behind you or God will bring you trouble all the next year. The World

Trade Center event is the first time I have seen this time of Elul in a worldwide situation. The whole world repented, except for the ones who committed the act. God will bring trouble on these men. There are many other areas where this event fits into the appointed times, but we will not look at these items at this time. Let's get back to the feasts.

The fall feasts are to bring the Israeli people to repentance and cleanse them from their sins. Thirty days before the new year, on the first of Tishri, a time of repentance starts. The Israeli people try to cleanse themselves of the sins for the previous year.

The new year starts on Rosh HaShanah. This is to remind the Israeli people that there are still ten days left before their sins are atoned for on Yom Kippur. The days between Rosh HaShanah and Yom Kippur are called the Days of Awe.

Five days after Yom Kippur, a feast of thanksgiving is held called Sukkot. This feast is very much like our Thanksgiving of today, except it lasts for seven days. This feast is to celebrate that Israel's sins are forgiven for another year.

Shemini Azeret is the eighth day of the Feast of Tabernacles. This literally means "the eighth day" in Hebrew. This day is a chance for the Israeli people who are putting on the Feast of Tabernacles to enjoy the feast before they must return to their homes.

Name	Month	Day	Comments
Rosh HaShanah	Tishri	1 - 2	Day of Judgement; Feast of Trumpets; Feast of No Man Knows the Day or The Hour.
Yom Kippur	Tishri	10	Day of Atonement; Holiest Day of the Year.
Sukkot	Tishri	15 - 21	Feast of Tabernacles; Pilgrimage Feast; Temporary Dwellings
Shemini Azeret	Tishri	22	The Eighth Day

Repentance

Teshuvah: This is the Hebrew word for repentance of sin, returning to God and to the right path.

Starting on the first day of the month of Elul, on the Hebrew calendar and ending on the tenth day of Tishri (Yom Kippur) is a forty-day season of repentance.

The month of Elul normally falls in our months of August and September. The temperature is always hot and tensions between people and God is high. This time of repentance is built into God's plan to help us get on the right path.

> 2 Peter 3:9
> *The Lord is not slow in keeping his promise, as some understand slowness. He is patient with you, not wanting anyone to perish, but everyone to come to repentance.*

> I Peter 3:9
> *Do not repay evil with evil or insult with insult, but with blessing, because to this you were called so that you may inherit a blessing.*

> Ezekiel 18:21-23
> *But if a wicked man turns away from all the sins he has committed and keeps all my decrees and does what is just and right, he will surely live; he will not die. None of the offenses he has committed will be remembered against him. Because of the righteous things he has done, he will live. Do I take any pleasure in the death of the wicked? Declares the Sovereign LORD. Rather, am I not pleased when they turn from their ways and live?*

> Ezekiel 18:30-32
> *Therefore, O House of Israel, I will judge you, each one according to his ways, declares the Sovereign LORD. Repent! Turn away from all your offenses; then sin will not be your downfall.*

Rid yourselves of all the offenses you have committed, and get a new heart and a new spirit. Why will you die, O House of Israel? For I take no pleasure in the death of anyone, declares the Sovereign LORD. Repent and live!

Sins committed against God and sins against man are dealt with differently. A sin offering was given for sins against God, and a guilt offering was used to restore man to man, before God.

Matthew 5:23-24
Therefore, if you are offering your gift at the altar and there remember that your brother has something against you, leave your gift there in front of the altar. First go and be reconciled to your brother; then come and offer your gift.

The season of Teshuvah is a time to look at our lives and restore relationships before Rosh HaShanah, the Day of Judgement. On this day the heavenly court sits reviewing each person.

Zephaniah 2:1-3
Gather together, gather together, O shameful nation, before the appointed time arrives and that day sweeps on like chaff, before the fierce anger of the LORD comes upon you, before the day of the Lord's wrath comes upon you. Seek the LORD, all you humble of the land, you who do what he commands. Seek righteousness, seek humility; perhaps you will be sheltered on the day of the Lord's anger.

Psalm 27 is said twice a day from the first of the month of Elul to the eighth day, Shemeni, Atzeret, the twenty-second day of the month of Tishri.

From the first of the month of Elul until the tenth of Tishri, the ram's horn is blown each morning following the morning prayers. This is a warning to each individual to turn back to God.

THE THREE BOOKS?

Does God have an eraser? He tells us in His Word that he will blot out the names of people in the Book of Life, if they don't accept His Son. I wonder if our names are written in pencil, or if they are written in ink. There might be three books, but the Bible itself only mentions two. The Book of Life and the book of the wicked. I hope he uses up all his erasers before he gets to my name.

Just kidding!

On the day of Rosh HaShanah each man is judged. God has three books opened. Those who have returned to God are written in the Book of the Righteous (Lamb's Book of Life.)

> John 14:6
> *Jesus answered, "I am the way and the truth and the life. No one comes to the Father except through me."*

> Revelation 3:5
> *"He who overcomes will, like them, be dressed in white. I will never blot out his name from the book of life, but will acknowledge his name before my Father and his angels."*

The others are divided into groups. The first of these groups are called the "Rashim," or the holy wicked. Their names are written into a book called "The Holy Wicked." The common people are given until Yom Kippur nine days later, to repent. If they repent, they are written into the "Book of The Righteous." If they don't repent, they are written into the "Book of the Holy Wicked."

The question arises: "What happens to someone who never got a chance to accept Jesus as Lord and Savior?" What book are they written into? They get another chance to receive Jesus as Lord after the thousand-year reign of Christ. We will look more at this later.

> Hosea 14:1-9
> *Return, O Israel, to the LORD your God. Your sins have been your downfall! Take words with you and return to the LORD.*

Say to him: Forgive all our sins and receive us graciously that we may offer the fruit of our lips. Assyria cannot save us; we will not mount war-horses. We will never again say "Our gods" to what our own hands have made, for in you the fatherless find compassion.

I will heal their waywardness and love them freely, for my anger has turned away from them. I will be like the dew to Israel; he will blossom like a lily. Like a cedar of Lebanon he will send down his roots; his young shoots will grow. His splendor will be like an olive tree, his fragrance like a cedar of Lebanon. Men will dwell again in his shade. He will flourish like the grain. He will blossom like a vine, and his fame will be like the wine from Lebanon. O Ephraim, what more have I to do with idols? I will answer him and care for him. I am like a green pine tree; your fruitfulness comes from me.

"Who is wise? He will realize these things. Who is discerning? He will understand them. The ways of the LORD are right; the righteous walk in them, but the rebellious stumble in them."

The Watchman

Most of the towns in ancient Israel had high walls around them to protect them from their enemies. The guards that kept watch on these walls, to warn the city about a possible attack, are called watchmen. The watchman is to sound the trumpet so that the people in the city know that trouble is coming. If the watchman doesn't sound the trumpet, he is liable for whatever happens, to anyone in the city. If he does sound the trumpet he has fulfilled his obligation and is not responsible for the actions of the people. Michael, in 1 Thessalonians 4:16, is the watchman.

> 1 Thessalonians 4:16
> For the Lord himself will come down from heaven, with a loud command, with the trumpet call of God, and the dead in Christ will rise first.

Ezekiel 33:1-6
The word of the LORD came to me: Son of man, speak to your countrymen and say to them: "When I bring the sword against a land, and the people of the land choose one of their men and make him their watchman, and he sees the sword coming against the land and blows the trumpet to warn the people, then if anyone hears the trumpet but does not take warning and the sword comes and takes his life, his blood will be on his own head. Since he heard the sound of the trumpet but did not take warning, his blood will be on his own head. If he had taken warning, he would have saved himself. But if the watchman sees the sword coming and does not blow the trumpet to warn the people and the sword comes and takes the life of one of them, that man will be taken away because of his sin, but I will hold the watchman accountable for his blood."

The watchman on the wall is to warn the people. The Day of Judgment is coming, along with the Kingdom of Heaven.

Ephesians 5:13-21
But everything exposed by the light becomes visible, for it is light that makes everything visible. This is why it is said: "Wake up, O Sleeper, rise from the dead, and Christ will shine on you."

Be very careful, then, how you live—not as unwise but as wise, making the most of every opportunity, because the days are evil. Therefore do not be foolish, but understand what the Lord's will is. Do not get drunk on wine, which leads to debauchery. Instead, be filled with the Spirit. Speak to one another with psalms, hymns and spiritual songs. Sing and make music in your heart to the Lord, always giving thanks to God the Father for everything, in the name of our Lord Jesus Christ. Submit to one another out of reverence for Christ.

Isaiah 18:3
All you people of the world, you who live on the earth, when a banner is raised on the mountains, you will see it, and when a trumpet sounds, you will hear it.

The banner is Jesus, and the trumpet is the trumpets on Rosh HaShanah.

Joel 2:1
Blow the trumpet in Zion; sound the alarm on my holy hill. Let all who live in the land tremble, for the day of the Lord is coming. It is close at hand...

Isaiah 26:1-3
In that day this song will be sung in the land of Judah: We have a strong city; God makes salvation its walls and ramparts. Open the gates that the righteous nation may enter, the nation that keeps faith. You will keep in perfect peace him whose mind is steadfast, because he trusts in you.

I Thessalonians 4:13-18
Brothers, we do not want you to be ignorant about those who fall asleep, or to grieve like the rest of men, who have no hope. We believe that Jesus died and rose again and so we believe that God will bring with Jesus those who have fallen asleep in him. According to the Lord's own word, we tell you that we who are still alive, who are left till the coming of the Lord, will certainly not precede those who have fallen asleep. For the Lord himself will come down from heaven, with a loud command, with the voice of the archangel and with the trumpet call of God, and the dead in Christ will rise first. After that, we who are still alive and are left will be caught up together with them in the clouds to meet the Lord in the air. And so we will be with the Lord forever. Therefore, encourage each other with these words.

The previous two Scriptures are pictures of the rapture of the Bride of Christ, the Church.

On the first day of the month of Elul, Moses carved out two new stone tablets, like the first ones that were broken. Moses carried them down the mountain forty days later on Yom Kippur. God atoned for the people's sin.

Earlier we said that the shofar was blown every day from the first of Elul to Tishri 10. The exception to this is the day before Rosh HaShanah. This is done to confuse Satan, who takes the blowing of the shofar as a sign that Rosh HaShanah has arrived. On the Day of Judgement, Satan brings his charges against the people. Satan becomes confused and doesn't know when to present his charges before the throne of God.

Before we look at Rosh HaShanah, we need to look at one more concept.

THE NEW MOON FESTIVAL

This calendar is a lunar one. The new moon festival is used to start off the New Year. Without this ceremony the Hebrew people would not know when the New Year started. Men would light fires on the tops of the mountains in Israel when the witnesses were established(see below), and the start of the new year was declared. This way everyone in the nation would know on what day the New Year started.

Rosh Chodesh plays an important role on Rosh HaShanah.

Rosh Chodesh means "head of the month" in Hebrew.

Actually the month starts when just a small sliver of the crescent moon is seen by two witnesses. These two witnesses travel to the temple to be interviewed by the Sanhedrin. When the testimony of the witnesses is established, the shofar is blown and the start of the Feast of Trumpets is declared.

If the sighting of the new moon is before sundown, say by only an hour or so, the trumpet is not blown until sundown. This is the start of a new day, the first day of the month.

Two days were reserved for the Feast of Trumpets because no one knows the day or the hour when the witnesses are established. Both days are considered one long day.

> Matthew 24:36-44
> *No, one knows about that day or hour, not even the angels in heaven, nor the Son, but only the Father. As it was in the days of Noah, so it will be at the coming of the Son of Man. For in the days before the flood, people were eating and drinking, marrying*

and giving in marriage, up to the day Noah entered the ark; and they knew nothing about what would happen until the flood came and took them all away. That is how it will be at the coming of the Son of Man. Two men will be in the field; one will be taken and the other left. Two women will be grinding with a hand mill; one will be taken and the other left.

Therefore keep watch, because you do not know on what day your Lord will come. But understand this: If the owner of the house had known at what time of night the thief was coming, he would have kept watch and would not have let his house be broken into. So you also must be ready, because the Son of Man will come at an hour when you do not expect him.

Rosh HaShanah is known as the "The Feast of No Man Knows the Day or The Hour."

Psalms 89:35-37
Once for all, I have sworn by my holiness—and I will not lie to David—that his line will continue forever and his throne endures before me like the sun; it will be established forever like the moon, the faithful witness in the sky.

The moon is a witness against us. When the moon is not visible—the new moon—it cannot testify against us.

Revelation 7:3
"Do not harm the land or the sea or the trees until we put a seal on the foreheads of the servants of our God."

In the ancient Hebrew language, the last letter of the alphabet was the letter *tov*. This letter looked like a cross. The *tov* is used as the seal that is placed on our foreheads, so that we are not hurt during the tribulation period. This seal shows that we belong to God. The current Hebrew symbol for the *tov* is a different symbol than the ancient language symbol. All believers in Christ are sealed with the cross.

We are ready to look at the feasts in the latter rain.

The Feast of Trumpets

This is not a jazz festival. I can just see Louie Armstrong and Dizzy Gallespie playing the trumpet for this feast. This would give new meaning to the term, "Feast of Trumpets." Who knows, maybe when that final trumpet sounds, one of these men will be playing it. One thing is for sure, in order the hear these two men again, we have to be in heaven. We serve a great God.

Rosh HaShanah means the "head of the year." This feast occurs on the first day of the Hebrew month of Tishri. When God created the universe, the first day was a Sunday. (See Appendix A)

> **Genesis 1:1**
> *In the beginning God created the heavens and the earth.*

> **Genesis 1:5**
> *God called the light "day," and the darkness he called "night." And there was evening, and there was morning—the first day.*

Many other major events in the Bible occurred on this day.

> **Genesis 8:13**
> *By the first day of the first month of Noah's six hundred and first year, the water had dried up from the earth. Noah then removed the covering from the ark and saw that the surface of the ground was dry.*

Joseph was let out of prison and placed in charge of Egypt. The rapture of the Church will take place. There are many more, and we'll look at some of them later.

<u>Names for Rosh HaShanah</u>
Head of the Year
Feast of Trumpets
Day of Judgement
Day of the Lord

Day No Man Knows the Day or the Hour
Wedding Day
Coronation Day

Isaiah 13:9-13
See, the day of the LORD is coming—a cruel day, with wrath and fierce anger—to make the land desolate and destroy the sinners within it. The stars of heaven and their constellations will not show their light. The rising sun will be darkened and the moon will not give its light. I will punish the world for its evil, the wicked for their sins. I will put an end to the arrogance of the haughty and will humble the pride of the ruthless. I will make man scarcer than pure gold, more rare than the gold of Ophir. Therefore, I will make the heavens tremble. The earth will shake from its place at the wrath of the LORD Almighty, in the day of his burning anger.

When the following passages are put together, you can see clearly the Salvation of God.

Zephaniah 2:3b
Seek the LORD, all you humble of the land, you who do what he commands. Seek righteousness, seek humility; <u>perhaps you will be sheltered on the day of the Lord's anger</u>.

Psalm 27:5
For in the day of trouble he will keep me safe in his dwelling; he will hide me in the shelter of his tabernacle and set me high upon a rock.

In Jerusalem the sounding of the trumpet has different meanings. The trumpets and shofar are used in different ways: they are used for temple services, a call to prepare for battle, and the Last Trump will be used for the wedding of believers to Jesus.

I Corinthians 14:8
Again, if the trumpet does not sound a clear call, who will get ready for battle?

Joshua 6:5
When you hear them sound a long blast on the trumpets, have all the people give a loud shout; then the wall of the city will collapse and the people will go up, every man straight in.

Is this a picture of what will happen when the trumpet is sounded on a future day. The people of God will give a loud shout and take the kingdom of heaven.

Isaiah 26:16-21
See. The LORD is coming out of his dwelling to punish the people of the earth for their Sins. The earth will disclose the blood shed upon her; she will conceal her slain no longer.

I Thessalonians 4:14-18
We believe that Jesus died and rose again and so we believe that God will bring with Jesus those who have fallen asleep in him. According to the Lord's own word, we tell you that we who are still alive, who are left till the coming of the Lord, will certainly not precede those who have fallen asleep. For the Lord himself will come down from heaven, with a loud command, with the voice of the archangel and with the trumpet call of God, and the dead in Christ will rise first. After that, we who are still alive and are left will be caught up together with them in the clouds to meet the Lord in the air. And so we will be with the Lord forever. Therefore, encourage each other with these words.

When the trumpet sounds on Rosh HaShanah, a wild goat horn is blown along with two silver trumpets. The goat horn is blown long and the trumpets short because the commandment of the day is for the shofar. Three sets of three trumpet blasts, each set consisting of a long blast, an even blast, a wavering blast, and a final *tekiah* are blown.

After the trumpet sounds on a given year, the Church ascends to meet the Lord in the air and we go into the marriage supper of the Lamb.

Revelation 11:1-3

I was given a reed like a measuring rod and was told, "Go and measure the temple of God and the altar, and count the worshipers there. But exclude the outer court; do not measure it, because it has been given to the Gentiles. They will trample on the holy city for 42 months. And I will give power to my two witnesses, and they will prophesy for 1,260 days, clothed in sackcloth."

The tribulation period begins on earth; in heaven a wedding is taking place. Psalm 45 is a picture of what is going on in heaven.

Psalm 45

For the director of music. To the tune of "Lilies." Of the Sons of Korah. A maskil. A wedding song. My heart is stirred by a noble theme as I recite my verses for the king; my tongue is the pen of a skillful writer.

You are the most excellent of men and your lips have been anointed with grace, since God has blessed you forever. Gird your sword upon your side, O mighty one; clothe yourself with splendor and majesty. In your majesty ride forth victoriously in behalf of truth, humility and righteousness; let your right hand display awesome deeds. Let your sharp arrows pierce the hearts of the king's enemies; let the nations fall beneath your feet. Your throne, O God, will last forever and ever; A scepter of justice will be the scepter of your kingdom. You love righteousness and hate wickedness; therefore God, your God, has set you above your companions by anointing you with the oil of joy. All your robes are fragrant with myrrh and aloes and cassias; from palaces adorned with ivory the music of the strings makes you glad. Daughters of kings are among your honored women; at your right hand is the royal bride in gold of Ophir.

Listen, O Daughter, consider and give ear: Forget your people and your father's house. The king is enthralled by your beauty; honor him, for he is your Lord. The Daughter of Tyre will come with a gift, and men of wealth will seek your favor.

All glorious is the princess within her chamber; her gown is interwoven with gold. In embroidered garments she is led to the king; her virgin companions follow her and are brought to you. They are led in with joy and gladness; they enter the palace of the king.

Your sons will take the place of your fathers; you will make them princes throughout the land. I will perpetuate your memory through all generations; therefore the nations will praise you forever and ever.

We can see below that Satan will try and change the set times and the laws of God. The calendar has been changed on man's time frame, from a lunar calendar to a solar calendar. The second level of time has not yet been changed. With the changing calendars, it is much more difficult to figure out our current location on God's calendar. We see what the evil one is trying to do to the people of the earth in Daniel 7.

Daniel 7:19-25

Then I wanted to know the true meaning of the fourth beast, which was different from all the others and most terrifying, with its iron teeth and bronze claws—the beast that crushed and devoured its victims and trampled underfoot whatever was left. I also wanted to know about the ten horns on its head and about the other horn that came up, before which three of them fell—the horn that looked more imposing than the others and that had eyes and a mouth that spoke boastfully. As I watched, this horn was waging war against the saints and defeating them, until the Ancient of Days came and pronounced judgment in favor of the saints of the Most High, and the time came when they possessed the kingdom.

He gave me this explanation: "The fourth beast is a fourth kingdom that will appear on earth. It will be different from all the other kingdoms and will devour the whole earth, trampling it down and crushing it. The ten horns are ten kings who will come from this kingdom. After them another king will arise, different from the earlier ones; he will subdue three kings. He will speak against the Most High and oppress his saints and try to change the set times and the laws. The saints will be handed over to him for a time, times and half a time.

The preceding Scripture (Daniel 7:19-25), is a picture of what is happening on earth while the wedding is taking place in heaven.

We will come back and look at the Feast of Trumpets, but we need to look at Yom Kippur first.

THE DAY OF ATONEMENT

Yom Kippur, the Day of Atonement is the holiest day of the year. This is the feast where God's Time Frame kicks in. Jesus fulfilled Yom Kippur on God's Time Frame. We will look at this in more detail and see how he fulfilled this feast later in the chapter. All of the major sections in this chapter, starting with the Day of Atonement and ending with the start of the Feast of Tabernacles, are part of the ceremonies for the Day of Atonement.

This is the only day of the year where the high priest could enter the Holy of Holies and sprinkle blood before the mercy seat of God. Aaron could enter the Holy of Holies at any time as long as it was Yom Kippur and the service was done properly. If Aaron wanted to enter the Holy of Holies on a day other than Yom Kippur he could do so by performing the Yom Kippur service properly.

Aaron had to perform Leviticus 16. None of Aaron's descendants could enter on a day other than on Yom Kippur. Jesus was one of Aaron's descendants, so he had to enter on Yom Kippur, and he did so on the "one thousand years are as a day" calendar.

> **Leviticus 16:32**
> *The priest who is anointed and ordained to succeed his father as high priest is to make atonement. He is to put on the sacred linen garments.*

Appendix A shows that Jesus fulfilled Yom Kippur on God's Time Frame. This way he would fulfill Hebrew law by entering the temple of God on the tenth of Tishri, on "the thousand years are as a day" calendar.

On this day, God grants or denies atonement for the coming year; for this reason Yom Kippur is also called the Day of Redemption.

> **Luke 23:34**
> *Jesus said, "Father, forgive them, for they do not know what they are doing," And they divided up his clothes by casting lots.*

Our sins are forgiven if we hold up Jesus as our banner. The judgement was postponed to see who would accept Jesus as their Savior.

Just like today in court, the first part of the case is to see if a crime was committed. Once the decision is given and someone is guilty, a date is set for sentencing. The guilty party then knows what price will have to be paid for the crime, and the sentence starts. God works on a similar idea—the only thing that can save us from God's judgement is to accept His Son as Savior and Lord.

This is the day where God purifies us from our errors. He forgives us and turns his ear toward us. On this day Moses came down from Mount Sinai with the second set of tablets. God forgave Israel for the sin of worshiping the golden calf.

Yom Kippur is the only feast where the high priest performs almost the entire service. Jesus was the sacrifice as well as the high priest at the same time. If Jesus had come during the fall rain and entered the Holy of Holies, and the high priest that held the earthly office was to enter the Holy of Holies, there would have been confusion. Which one would really have been the high priest? So Jesus came during God's Time Frame and fulfilled Yom Kippur.

Let's look at the Mishnah:

The Laws of Yom Kippur

We will try and go through the major points of the festival, comparing the Mishnah to the Bible. There are many points about the law that we will not cover here. The law is much too detailed to cover every fulfillment of prophecy. We will look at some of the laws that are easy to notice in Scripture. Some of the other laws will require much more research to show them properly, and a much larger book to explain them. Maybe next time.

Jesus Establishes His Residence

On the tenth day of Nisan, the seventh month of the civil calendar, the separating of the high priest from his home to the official's chamber begins.

Yoma 1:1a
"Seven days before Yom Kippur they sequester the Kohen Gadol from his house to the official's chamber and they prepare another Kohen as his substitute, lest he becomes disqualified."

Artscroll
Gemara(80)
"The official's chamber used to be called the Prince's chamber, but when the high priest position was later bought and sold, it became the official's chamber."
  "Seven days before Yom Kippur, the high priest rides a donkey into Jerusalem."

Matthew 21:1-11
As they approached Jerusalem and came to Bethphage on the Mount of Olives, Jesus sent two disciples, saying to them, "Go to the village ahead of you, and at once you will find a donkey tied there, with her colt by her. Untie them and bring them to me. If anyone says anything to you, tell him that the Lord needs them, and he will send them right away."
  This took place to fulfill what was spoken through the prophet: Say to the Daughter of Zion, "See, your king comes to you, gentle and riding on a donkey, on a colt, the foal of a donkey."
  The disciples went and did as Jesus had instructed them. They brought the donkey and the colt, placed their cloaks on them, and Jesus sat on them. A very large crowd spread their cloaks on the road, while others cut branches from the trees and spread them on the road. The crowds that went ahead of him and those that followed shouted, "Hosanna to the Son of David!" "Blessed is he who comes in the name of the Lord!" "Hosanna in the highest!"

> When Jesus entered Jerusalem, the whole city was stirred and asked, "Who is this?" The crowds answered, "This is Jesus, the prophet from Nazareth in Galilee."

Yoma 1:1 (Footnote)
"The purpose of establishing residence on the temple mount is to separate the high priest from his wife, so that he would not become unclean. It was not necessary to stay in the prince's chamber just in the vicinity of the temple mount."

Let's look at Jesus' actions in establishing his residence.

Matthew 21:12-13
Jesus entered the temple area and drove out all who were buying and selling there. He overturned the tables of the moneychangers and the benches of those selling doves. "It is written," he said to them, 'My house will be called a house of prayer,' but you are making it a 'den of robbers.'"

Jesus established his house by saying, "My house, is a house of prayer."
If we roll back and look at Yoma 1:1, another Kohen is prepared as his substitute if he becomes disqualified.

Psalm 98:1
A psalm. Sing to the LORD a new song, for he has done marvelous things; his right hand and his holy arm have worked salvation for him.

In heaven Jesus is at the right hand of the Father, he is currently the backup high priest. On earth Jesus is our high priest. So who is Jesus' backup, the priest at Jesus' right hand on earth? I believe Peter is the backup high priest, and he is the only person besides Jesus to walk on water.

Matthew 14:28-30
"Lord, if it's you," Peter replied, "tell me to come to you on the water." "Come," he said. Then Peter got down out of the boat,

walked on the water and came toward Jesus. But when he saw the wind, he was afraid and, beginning to sink, cried out, "Lord, save me!?"

Jesus also named Peter. *Peter* means "rock" in Hebrew.

John 1:42
And he brought him to Jesus. Jesus looked at him and said, "You are Simon Son of John. You will be called Cephas" (which, when translated, is Peter).

The High Priest Atones for His House

The high priest has to have a wife, so he can atone for the sins of his household. If the high priest's wife dies during the seven days leading up to the feast, he could not meet the requirements and fulfill Scripture.

Yoma 1:1b
"R'Yehudah says: 'They also prepare another wife for him, lest his wife die, for it is said: and he shall make atonement for himself and for His House (Leviticus 16:6). His house: that is his wife. They said to him: 'If so there is no end to the matter.' "

Leviticus 16:6
Aaron is to offer the bull for his own sin offering to make atonement for himself and his household.

A backup wife is set up just in case the first wife dies. A condition is put into the marriage contract that states if the first wife dies, the backup becomes the high priest's wife. If his first wife doesn't die, the backup is released from the commitment.

Israel is many times pictured as the "fig tree." The Church is referred to as the "coming Bride of Jesus."

Matthew 21:19
"Do you hear what these children are saying?" they asked him. "Yes," replied Jesus, have you never read, 'From the lips of children and infants you have ordained praise?"

Seeing a fig tree by the road, He went up to it but found nothing on it except leaves. Then He said to it, "May you never bear fruit again!" Immediately the tree withered.

If the first wife dies, it is several days after Yom Kippur before the high priest can marry again. Hebrew weddings traditionally take place on our Wednesday night, Hebrew Thursday night. Going back to appendix A, we can see that we are in the early part of Thursday night, close to the wedding with Jesus.

Revelation 21:9b
One of the seven angels who had the seven bowls full of the seven last plagues came and said to me, "<u>Come, I will show you the bride, the wife of the Lamb</u>."

Matthew 22:1-14
Jesus spoke to them again in parables, saying: "The kingdom of heaven is like a king who prepared a wedding banquet for his son. He sent his servants to those who had been invited to the banquet to tell them to come, but they refused to come.

"Then he sent some more servants and said, 'Tell those who have been invited that I have prepared my dinner: My oxen and fattened cattle have been butchered, and everything is ready. Come to the wedding banquet.'

"But they paid no attention and went off—one to his field, another to his business. The rest seized his servants, mistreated them and killed them. The king was enraged. He sent his army and destroyed those murderers and burned their city.

"Then he said to his servants, 'The wedding banquet is ready, but those I invited did not deserve to come. Go to the street corners and invite to the banquet anyone you find.' So the servants went out into the streets and gathered all the people

they could find, both good and bad, and the wedding hall was filled with guests.

"But when the king came in to see the guests, he noticed a man there who was not wearing wedding clothes. 'Friend,' he asked, 'how did you get in here without wedding clothes?' The man was speechless.

"Then the king told the attendants, 'Tie him hand and foot, and throw him outside, into the darkness, where there will be weeping and gnashing of teeth.' For many are invited, but few are chosen."

Anyone can become a part of the Bride of Christ by accepting Jesus as Savior and Lord.

The High Priest's Portion

Jesus shed his blood for us as our high priest. So what is his portion for this great sacrifice?

Jesus became the servant of mankind for giving his life on the cross. God has made him the greatest person in heaven, but he also received a portion on earth (see below).

> Yoma 1:2
> *"On all of these seven days he throws the blood, burns the incense, prepares the lamps, and offers the head and the hind leg. On all the other days (of the year), if he wishes to offer any sacrifice, he may offer it. For the Kohen Gadol has the first right to offer and the first right to take a portion."*

I haven't been able to find how the blood is thrown all seven days. Jesus did shed his blood seven different ways during holy week.

Prayers going up to heaven: Several times while in prayer, I have noticed a wonderful smell. I believe that this is incense that is rising up to the throne room of God. The smell is so wonderful, like fragrant flowers, it makes you want to stay in His presence. We serve a glorious Lord.

> Psalms 18:28
> *You, O LORD, keep my lamp burning; my God turns my darkness into light.*

The lamps that are lit are the saints. I could never understand what the Bible was saying when the believers in the Lord were described as lamps. One night while I was driving up Route 395 to Lone Pine, California, I was praising and talking to the Lord, and the power of the Holy Spirit fell. The anointing was so strong in my truck that I thought the road signs would blow over. Then it happened—the presence of the Lord came down on me. The whole inside of my truck was lit up like I had a spotlight on top of my head. My face was radiant like Moses' when he came down from the mountain. What a wonderful experience with the Lord. I believe this is what the Word means when it talks about the saints being lamps. He wants us to be lit and ready to do His will at all times.

The head and hind leg represent the evening sacrifice.

The high priest has the first right to offer and the first right to take a portion. Jesus offered himself as the sacrifice, and his portion of land is in Ezekiel.

> Ezekiel 45:1
> *When you allot the land as an inheritance, you are to present to the LORD a portion of the land as a sacred district, 25,000 cubits long and 20,000 cubits wide; the entire area will be holy.*

The Upper Chamber

Here we see Jesus preparing for the Passover and also entering the Avtina's family's upper chamber. We can see the large upper room in Mark's gospel.

> Yoma 1:4-5a
> *"During the entire seven day period, they did not withhold food and drink from him, but on the eve of Yom Kippur toward nightfall they did not let him eat much, because food induces sleep. The*

sages of the court put him in the custody of the sages of the priesthood who took him up to the Avtinas Family's upper chamber, adjured him took their leave and went their way."

Mark 14:12-16
On the first day of the Feast of Unleavened Bread, when it was customary to sacrifice the Passover lamb, Jesus' disciples asked him, "Where do you want us to go and make preparations for you to eat the Passover?"

So he sent two of his disciples, telling them, "Go into the city, and a man carrying a jar of water will meet you. Follow him. Say to the owner of the house he enters, 'The Teacher asks: Where is my guest room, where I may eat the Passover with my disciples?' He will show you a large upper room furnished and ready. Make preparations for us there."

The disciples left, went into the city and found things just as Jesus had told them. So they prepared the Passover.

Let's look at Jesus washing the disciples' feet. We have an entry in the Mishnah about a laver that was created to wash up to twelve priests' feet. So this must have been part of the Yom Kippur ceremony.

Yoma 3:10a
"Ben Katin made twelve spouts for the laver, for it (formerly had only two): he also made a machine for the laver so that its water should not become unfit by remaining overnight."

John 13:3-7
Jesus knew that the Father had put all things under his power, and that he had come from God and was returning to God; so he got up from the meal, took off his outer clothing, and wrapped a towel around his waist. After that, he poured water into a basin and began to wash his disciples' feet, drying them with the towel that was wrapped around him. He came to Simon Peter, who said to him, "Lord, are you going to wash my feet?" Jesus replied, "You do not realize now what I am doing, but later you will understand."

Yoma 1:6a
"If he was a scholar, he lectured; but if not scholars would lecture before him. If he was accustomed to read (Scripture), he would read; but if not, they would read to him."

Jesus lectured the disciples during the Last Supper. His lecture is found in John 13 through 17 and includes his Mount of Olives prayers.

The Mount of Olives

After the Last Supper was completed, Jesus took the disciples out to the Mount of Olives to pray. This is where he was to be turned over to the Jews.

Mark 14:26
When they had sung a hymn, they went out to the Mount of Olives.

At a place called Gethsemane, Jesus' disciples were supposed to help keep him awake, but as we can see, it was the other way around.

Yoma 1:7
"If he wished to doze, young men of the priesthood snapped before him with the index finger, and they said to him, 'My Lord, Kohen Gadol, stand up and cool off once on the floor; And they kept him busy until the time for slaughtering arrived."

Mark 14:32-42
They went to a place called Gethsemane, and Jesus said to his disciples, "Sit here while I pray." He took Peter, James and John along with him, and he began to be deeply distressed and troubled. "My soul is overwhelmed with sorrow to the point of death," he said to them. "Stay here and keep watch."

Going a little farther, he fell to the ground and prayed that if possible the hour might pass from him. "Abba, Father," he said, "everything is possible for you. Take this cup from me. Yet not what I will, but what you will."

Then he returned to his disciples and found them sleeping. "Simon," he said to Peter, "are you asleep? Could you not keep watch for one hour? Watch and pray so that you will not fall into temptation. The spirit is willing, but the body is weak."

Once more he went away and prayed the same thing. When he came back, he again found them sleeping, because their eyes were heavy. They did not know what to say to him.

Returning the third time, he said to them, "Are you still sleeping and resting? Enough! The hour has come. Look, the Son of Man is betrayed into the hands of sinners. Rise! Let us go! Here comes my betrayer!"

We see Peter and John following Jesus through the trials that he was put though by Caiaphas, Herod, and Pilate. We also see Peter and John following Jesus—which one will win the first lot?

Yoma 2:1b-2
"If two of them were even, the administrator would say to them, 'Put out a finger.' What did they put out? One or two, but they did not put out a thumb in the Temple."

"It once happened that two were even as they ran ascended the ramp, and one of them pushed his colleague; he fell and his leg was broken. Once the court realized that there was a danger, they instituted that they not remove from the altar except by lot."

"There were four lots there; this is the first lot."

Matthew 26:58
But Peter followed him at a distance, right up to the courtyard of the high priest. He entered and sat down with the guards to see the outcome.

The Altar

Here we see a play on words. Jesus was taken to the house of the high priest, which in this case could have been the temple. A fire was lit in the middle of the courtyard, a picture of the altar in the temple of the Lord.

Luke 22:54-56
Then seizing him, they led him away and took him into the house of the high priest. Peter followed at a distance. But when they kindled a fire in the middle of the courtyard and sat down together, Peter sat down with them. A servant girl saw him seated there in the firelight. She looked closely at him and said, "This man was with him."

John 18:15
Simon Peter and another disciple were following Jesus. Because this disciple was known to the high priest, he went with Jesus into the high priest's courtyard.

Yoma 2:3a
"The second lot was (to determine) who slaughters."

Yoma 2:3–3:7 goes into more detail as to the things that are done to our Lord. We see in Scripture the lot being cast for his life. Jesus goes before Caiaphas, Herod and Pilate and is mocked and beaten by guards. We know that Pilate wins this lot. He is the one who slaughters the Lord.

Luke 23:13-17
Pilate called together the chief priests, the rulers and the people, and said to them, "You brought me this man as one who was inciting the people to rebellion. I have examined him in your presence and have found no basis for your charges against him. Neither has Herod, for he sent him back to us; as you can see, he has done nothing to deserve death. Therefore, I will punish him and then release him. (For of necessity he must release one unto them at the feast.)"

The Scapegoat

As we look at Yoma 4:1, we see the scapegoat. This is one of the major points that leads me in this study. The scapegoat ceremony doesn't fit anywhere but in Yom Kippur. It always seems so strange to see it in the middle of the Spring Feasts.

The goat that was to be sacrificed for the sins of Israel is Jesus. Pilate was selected as the winner of the lot; he was the one who was selected to do the sacrifice. Pilate had Jesus flogged, then handed him over to be crucified. The goat that was to carry the sins of Israel into the wilderness was Barabbas.

Yoma 4:1a
"He snatched from the lottery box and picked up two lots; one had, 'for HaShem' inscribed on it and one had for Azazel inscribed on it."

"The lot that had been set up for HaShem (The Name) was to be sacrificed for the sins of Israel and for the high priest and his family."

"The goat that was to go to Azazel, the wilderness was to carry all Israel's sins into the wilderness where they would be done away with."

"A red cloth was tied to the goat that was to go into the wilderness. This goat was to be led out into the wilderness and thrown off a cliff, when the goat dies the cloth turns from red to white. A piece of the same cloth was tied to a post at the temple. This piece of cloth also turns white when the goat dies. So everyone knows the sins of Israel are atoned for."

Yoma 4:2a
"He tied a strip of red wool to the head of the he-goat which was sent to Azazel and stood it facing its destination. And on the he-goat that was to be slaughtered, he tied a strip around its neck."

Isaiah 1:8
"Come now, let us reason together," says the LORD. "Though your sins are like scarlet, they shall be as white as snow; though they are red as crimson, they shall be like wool."

The King's Household

Any member of a king's household can walk around the palace in confidence. If we were to go to the White House, we would be very careful while walking through it. A child of the president would be totally at ease while playing in the rooms. Jesus is a member of the king's household, and so are we!

> Yoma 4:5a
> "Every day the Kohanim go up (to the top of the altar) along the east side of the ramp and go down along its west, but today the Kohen Gadol goes up in the middle and descends in the middle."

This is a picture of Jesus entering the Holy of Holies right down the center. The high priest normally has to walk around the temple curtain. But today the high priest is conducting himself on the altar like a member of the king's household.

> Matthew 27:51
> *At that moment the curtain of the temple was torn in two from top to bottom. The earth shook and the rocks split.*

This step of the ceremony happens later on in the service. This is just a picture of Jesus tearing the curtain.

In Yoma 5:3-6, we see the blood of the sacrifices being applied to the curtain in a whipping motion.

> Yoma 5:3a
> "He took the blood from one who was stirring it. He entered the place he had (previously) entered; stood in the place he had stood and sprinkled from it one (time) upward and seven (times) downward. But he did not aim in sprinkling either above or below, rather like one who whips."

> Matthew 27:26
> *Then he released Barabbas to them. But he had Jesus flogged, and handed him over to be crucified.*

Jesus' crucifixion is the end of the scapegoat ceremony.

Yoma 5:7 states that all the steps of the Yom Kippur ceremony up to this point have to be in the correct order for the atonement of our sins to be valid.

Yoma 5:7a
"The entire Yom Kippur service that has been listed in sequence, if he advanced one service before another, he has accomplished nothing."

Guards Falling in Fear

This section of the law is broken up into two sections. The first section takes place while Jesus was on the cross, and the second section happens as he is raised from the dead.

Yoma 6:2b
"The Kohanim and the people who were standing in the courtyard, when they heard the ineffable name coming from the Kohen Gadol's mouth, they would kneel and prostrate themselves and fall upon their faces, and say, 'Blessed be the name—the glory of His Kinship—forever and ever.'"

Matthew 27:45-54
From the sixth hour until the ninth hour darkness came over all the land. About the ninth hour Jesus cried out in a loud voice, "Eloi, Eloi, Lama Sabachthani?"—which means "My God, my God, why have you forsaken me?"

When some of those standing there heard this, they said, "He's calling Elijah."

Immediately one of them ran and got a sponge. He filled it with wine vinegar, put it on a stick, and offered it to Jesus to drink. The rest said, "Now leave him alone. Let's see if Elijah comes to save him."

And when Jesus had cried out again in a loud voice, he gave up his spirit.

At that moment the curtain of the temple was torn in two from top to bottom. The Earth shook and the rocks split.

The tombs broke open and the bodies of many holy people who had died were raised to life. They came out of the tombs, and after Jesus' resurrection they went into the holy city and appeared to many people.

> When the centurion and those with him who were guarding
> Jesus saw the earthquake and all that had happened, they were
> terrified, and exclaimed, "Surely he was the son of God!"

I believe the name that Jesus said was the sacred name of God that only the high priest could say once a year on Yom Kippur. No one on earth can say this name that consists of forty-two Hebrew letters. Only the high priest can say this name when he is filled with the power of the Holy Spirit once a year on Yom Kippur.

From this point on, the Day of Atonement ceremony is put on hold until it is time for Jesus to be raised from the dead.

We see the guards falling down in fear in Matthew 28. This step was mentioned in Yoma 6:2b. This was the next step in the ceremony after Jesus said "The Name." Even though it was several days after the Lord spoke "The Name," the next step in the ceremony was the guards prostrating themselves around the tomb when he came out of the grave.

> Matthew 28:2-4
> There was a violent earthquake, for an angel of the Lord came
> down from heaven and, going to the tomb, rolled back the stone
> and sat on it. His appearance was like lightning, and his clothes
> were white as snow. The guards were so afraid of him that they
> shook and became like dead men.

The Road to Emmaus

In Yoma 7:1, we see the Lord in his linen clothing, teaching the men on the road to Emmaus.

Emmaus means "hot bath" in Hebrew. Was Jesus going to Emmaus to take a hot bath? The high priest had to immerse himself in water several different times before entering into the Holy of Holies to fulfill the laws for the Day of Atonement.

> Yoma 7:1
> "The Kohen Gadol came to read. If he wished to read (wearing)
> his linen vestments. He may read; and if not, he would read while
> wearing his own white robe."

"The attendant of the synagogue takes a Torah scroll and gives it to the head of the synagogue; the head of the synagogue gives it to the deputy (Kohen Gadol); and the deputy gives it to the Kohen Gadol. The Kohen Gadol stands up, accepts (the scroll) and reads while standing."

"He reads (from) "Acharei Mos" (Leviticus 16) and (the portion that begins) "But on the tenth" (Leviticus 23:26 - 32) then he rolls up the Torah scroll, put it in his bosom, and says, 'More than I have read to you is written here'; and he recites from his heart the Book of Numbers, beginning, 'On the tenth'(Numbers 29:7-11)."

"Then he recites over it eight benedictions: for the Torah; for the (sacrificial) service; for the Thanksgiving; for the forgiveness of sins; for the temple separately; for Israel separately; for Jerusalem separately; for the Kohanim separately; and for the rest of the prayer."

Following are the Scriptures that were mentioned in Yoma 7:1 about Yom Kippur:

Leviticus 23:26-32
The LORD said to Moses, "The tenth day of this seventh month is the Day of Atonement. Hold a sacred assembly and deny yourselves, and present an offering made to the LORD by fire. Do no work on that day, because it is the Day of Atonement, when atonement is made for you before the LORD your God. Anyone who does not deny himself on that day must be cut off from his people. I will destroy from among his people anyone who does any work on that day. You shall do no work at all. This is to be a lasting ordinance for the generations to come, wherever you live. It is a Sabbath of rest for you, and you must deny yourselves. From the evening of the ninth day of the month until the following evening you is to observe your Sabbath."

Numbers 29:7-11
"On the tenth day of this seventh month hold a sacred assembly. You must deny yourselves and do no work. Present as an aroma

pleasing to the LORD a burnt offering of one young bull, one ram and seven male lambs a year old, all without a defect. With the bull prepare a grain offering of three-tenths of an ephah of fine flour mixed with oil; with the ram, two-tenths; and with each of the seven lambs, one-tenth. Include one male goat as a sin offering, in addition to the sin offering for atonement and the regular burnt offering with its grain offering, and their drink offerings."

There are so many points to be made about Yoma 7:1, and I don't know where to begin. We see Jesus teaching two of his followers along the road to Emmaus, while wearing his own white robe. The linen strips were lying by themselves in the tomb.

Luke 24:13-25
Now that same day two of them were going to a village called Emmaus, about seven miles from Jerusalem. They were talking with each other about everything that had happened. As they talked and discussed these things with each other, Jesus himself came up and walked along with them; but they were kept from recognizing him.

He asked them, "What are you discussing together as you walk along?" They stood still, their faces downcast. One of them, named Cleopas, asked him, "Are you only a visitor to Jerusalem and do not know the things that have happened there in these days?" "What things?" he asked. "About Jesus of Nazareth," they replied. "He was a prophet, powerful in word and deed before God and all the people. The chief priests and our rulers handed him over to be sentenced to death, and they crucified him; but we had hoped that he was the one who was going to redeem Israel. And what is more, it is the third day since all this took place. In addition, some of our women amazed us. They went to the tomb early this morning but didn't find his body. They came and told us that they had seen a vision of angels, who said he was alive. Then some of our companions went to the tomb and found it just as the women had said, but him they did not see."

He said to them, "How foolish you are, and how slow of heart to believe all that the prophets have spoken!"

Luke 24:12
Peter, however, got up and ran to the tomb. Bending over, he saw the strips of linen lying by themselves, and he went away, wondering to himself what had happened.

The second paragraph of Yoma 7:1, we need to jump ahead to the book of Revelation.

Revelation 5:1-5
Then I saw in the right hand of him who sat on the throne a scroll with writing on both sides and sealed with seven seals. And I saw a mighty angel proclaiming in a loud voice, "Who is worthy to break the seals and open the scroll? But no one in heaven or on earth or under the earth could open the scroll or even look inside it. I wept and wept because no one was found who was worthy to open the scroll or look inside. Then one of the elders said to me, "Do not weep! See, the Lion of the tribe of Judah, the Root of David, has triumphed. He is able to open the scroll and its seven seals."

As we look at the third paragraph of Yoma 7:1, we can see what Jesus was teaching the men along the road to Emmaus. Go back and look at Luke 24:27:

"And beginning with Moses and all the Prophets, he explained to them what was said in all the Scriptures concerning himself."

Jesus explained all the Scriptures concerning Himself. The Scriptures are listed in the third paragraph of Yoma 7:1.
The first Scripture is Leviticus 16:

The LORD spoke to Moses after the death of the two sons of Aaron who died when they approached the LORD. The LORD said to Moses: "Tell your brother Aaron not to come whenever he chooses into the Most Holy Place behind the curtain in front of the atonement cover on the ark, or else he will die, because I appear in the cloud over the atonement cover.

This is how Aaron is to enter the sanctuary area: with a young bull for a sin offering and a ram for a burnt offering. He is to put on the sacred linen tunic, with linen undergarments next to his body; he is to tie the linen sash around him and put on the linen turban. These are sacred garments; so he must bathe himself with water before he puts them on. From the Israelite community he is to take two male goats for a sin offering and a ram for a burnt offering.

Aaron is to offer the bull for his own sin offering to make atonement for himself and his household. Then he is to take the two goats and present them before the LORD at the entrance to the Tent of Meeting. He is to cast lots for the two goats—one lot for the LORD and the other for the scapegoat. Aaron shall bring the goat whose lot falls to the LORD and sacrifice it for a sin offering. But the goat chosen by lot as the scapegoat shall be presented alive before the LORD to be used for making atonement by sending it into the desert as a scapegoat.

Aaron shall bring the bull for his own sin offering to make atonement for himself and his household, and he is to slaughter the bull for his own sin offering. He is to take a censer full of burning coals from the altar before the LORD and two handfuls of finely ground fragrant incense and take them behind the curtain. He is to put the incense on the fire before the LORD, and the smoke of the incense will conceal the atonement cover above the Testimony, so that he will not die. He is to take some of the bull's blood and with his finger sprinkle it on the front of the atonement cover; then he shall sprinkle some of it with his finger seven times before the atonement cover.

He shall then slaughter the goat for the sin offering for the people and take its blood behind the curtain and do with it as he did with the bull's blood: He shall sprinkle it on the atonement cover and in front of it. In this way he will make atonement for the Most Holy Place because of the uncleanness and rebellion of the Israelites, whatever their sins have been. He is to do the same for the Tent of Meeting, which is among them in the midst of their uncleanness. No one is to be in the Tent of Meeting from the time Aaron goes in to make atonement in the Most Holy Place until he comes out, having made atonement for himself, his household and the whole community of Israel.

Then he shall come out to the altar that is before the LORD and make atonement for it. He shall take some of the bull's blood and some of the goat's blood and put it on all the horns of the altar. He shall sprinkle some of the blood on it with his finger seven times to cleanse it and to consecrate it from the uncleanness of the Israelites. When Aaron has finished making atonement for the Most Holy Place, the Tent of Meeting and the altar, he shall bring forward the live goat. He is to lay both hands on the head of the live goat and confess over it all the wickedness and rebellion of the Israelites—all their sins—and put them on the goat's head. He shall send the goat away into the desert in the care of a man appointed for the task. The goat will carry on itself all their sins to a solitary place; and the man shall release it in the desert.

Then Aaron is to go into the Tent of Meeting and take off the linen garments he put on before he entered the Most Holy Place, and he is to leave them there. He shall bathe himself with water in a holy place and put on his regular garments. Then he shall come out and sacrifice the burnt offering for himself and the burnt offering for the people, to make atonement for himself and for the people. He shall also burn the fat of the sin offering on the altar.

The man who releases the goat as a scapegoat must wash his clothes and bathe him- self with water; afterward he may come into the camp. The bull and the goat for the sin offerings, whose blood was brought into the Most Holy Place to make atonement, must be taken outside the camp; their hides, flesh and offal are to be burned up. The man who burns them must wash his clothes and bathe himself with water; afterward he may come into the camp.

This is to be a lasting ordinance for you: On the tenth day of the seventh month you must deny yourselves and not do any work—whether native-born or an alien living among you—because on this day atonement will be made for you, to cleanse you. Then, before the LORD, you will be clean from all your sins. It is a Sabbath of rest, and you must deny yourselves; it is a lasting ordinance. The priest who is anointed and ordained to succeed his father as high priest is to make atonement. He is to put on the sacred linen garments and make atonement for the Most Holy Place, for the Tent of Meeting and the altar, and for the priests and all the people of the community.

"This is to be a lasting ordinance for you: Atonement is to be made once a year for all the sins of the Israelites." And it was done, as the LORD commanded Moses.

These Scriptures are the laws for services on the Day of Atonement. The second Scripture, Leviticus 23:16-32, is also for the Day of Atonement.

Leviticus 23:16-32
"Count off fifty days up to the day after the seventh Sabbath, and then present an offering of new grain to the LORD. From wherever you live, bring two loaves made of two-tenths of an ephah of fine flour, baked with yeast, as a wave offering of first fruits to the LORD. Present with this bread seven male lambs, each a year old and without defect, one young bull and two rams. They will be a burnt offering to the LORD, together with their grain offerings and drink offerings—an offering made by fire, an aroma pleasing to the LORD. Then sacrifice one male goat for a sin offering and two lambs, each a year old, for a fellowship offering. The priest is to wave the two lambs before the LORD as a wave offering, together with the bread of the first fruits. They are a sacred offering to the LORD for the priest. On that same day you are to proclaim a sacred assembly and do no regular work. This is to be a lasting ordinance for the generations to come, wherever you live. When you reap the harvest of your

land, do not reap to the very edges of your field or gather the gleanings of your harvest. Leave them for the poor and the alien. I am the LORD your God.

The LORD said to Moses, "Say to the Israelites: 'On the first day of the seventh month you are to have a day of rest, a sacred assembly commemorated with trumpet blasts. Do no regular work, but present an offering made to the LORD by fire.'"

The LORD said to Moses, "The tenth day of this seventh month is the Day of Atonement. Hold a sacred assembly and deny yourselves, and present an offering made to the LORD by fire. Do no work on that day, because it is the Day of Atonement, when atonement is made for you before the LORD your God. Anyone who does not deny himself on that day must be cut off from his people. I will destroy from among his people anyone who does any work on that day. You shall do no work at all. This is to be a lasting ordinance for the generations to come, wherever you live. It is a Sabbath of rest for you, and you must deny yourselves. From the evening of the ninth day of the month until the following evening you are to observe your Sabbath."

The final Scripture, Numbers 29:7-11, is also on the Day of Atonement.

Numbers 29:7-11

"On the tenth day of this seventh month hold a sacred assembly. You must deny yourselves and do no work. Present as an aroma pleasing to the LORD a burnt offering of one young bull, one ram and seven male lambs a year old, all without defect.

"With the bull prepare a grain offering of three-tenths of an ephah of fine flour mixed with oil; with the ram, two-tenths; and with each of the seven lambs, one-tenth. Include one male goat as a sin offering, in addition to the sin offering for atonement and the regular burnt offering with its grain offering, and their drink offerings."

We see several of the items mentioned in paragraph four of Yoma 7:1 in John 24:45-49.

> John 24:45-49
> *Then he opened their minds so they could understand the Scriptures. He told them, "This is what is written: 'The Christ will suffer and rise from the dead on the third day, and repentance and forgiveness of sins will be preached in his name to all nations, beginning at Jerusalem.' You are witnesses of these things. I am going to send you what my Father has promised; but stay in the city until you have been clothed with power from on high."*

> Yoma 7:2
> *"One who sees the Kohen Gadol when he reads cannot see the ox and the he-goat as they are burned. (And) One who sees the ox and the he-goat as they are burned cannot see the Kohen Gadol when he reads; not because he may not, but because the distance (between them) was great, and both services were performed at the same time."*

If we go back to Yoma 7:1, we see Jesus teaching on the road to Emmaus, while the sacrifices were being placed on the altar in the temple. The distance between Emmaus and the Temple was too great for anyone to see both Jesus teaching and the altar of the Temple, at the same time.

Cooking a Feast

This is the last point in the Day of Atonement ceremony. The high priest is to cook a feast for the other priests at his home.

> Yoma 7:4
> *"He washed his hands and feet, undressed, went down (into the Mikuen) and immersed (himself), and came up and dried himself. They brought him white (linen) vestments; he dressed, and washed his hands and feet."*
>
> *"He entered (the Holy of Holies) to take out the ladle and the shouel."*

"He washed his hands and feet, undressed, went down immersed, came up, and dries himself."

"They brought him golden vestments; he dressed, washed his hands and feet. And entered (the Holy) to burn the afternoon incense and light the lamps."

"Then he washed his hands and feet and undressed. They brought him his personal clothing and he dressed. Then they accompanied him to his house and he made a feast, for his friends for having left the Temple safely."

The term *Mikuen* in Yoma 7:4 is a ritual bath that cleans both the body and spirit. After touching a dead body or unclean animal, a man or woman is to take a ritual bath. Jesus was on his way to take a bath at Emmaus, after being dead. I wonder how the Rabbis would judge this situation. I'm glad I'm not a Rabbi!

We see one of the times when Jesus was to enter the Holy of Holies in John 20:17:

> John 20:17
> Jesus said, "Do not hold on to me, for I have not yet returned to the Father. Go instead to my brothers and tell them, 'I am returning to my Father and your Father, to my God and your God.'"

If Mary had touched Jesus at that time, He would have become unclean and would not have been able to enter the Holy of Holies. We see Jesus at least four times on Resurrection Sunday. He was in and out of the temple several times.

The last paragraph of Yoma 7:4 really stands out. We see Jesus along the Sea of Galilee cooking a feast for his friends. The Sea of Galilee was Jesus' home.

> John 21:5-13
> He called out to them, "Friends, haven't you any fish?" "No," they answered. He said, "Throw your net on the right side of the boat and you will find some." When they did, they were unable

> to haul the net in because of the large number of fish. Then the
> disciple whom Jesus loved said to Peter, "It is the Lord!" As soon
> as Simon Peter heard him say, "It is the Lord," he wrapped his
> outer garment around him (for he had taken it off) and jumped
> into the water. The other disciples followed in the boat, towing
> the net full of fish, for they were not far from shore, about a hundred yards. When they landed, they saw a fire of burning coals
> there with fish on it, and some bread. Jesus said to them, "Bring
> some of the fish you have just caught." Simon Peter climbed
> aboard and dragged the net ashore. It was full of large fish, 153,
> but even with so many the net was not torn. Jesus said to them,
> "Come and have breakfast." None of the disciples dared ask him,
> "Who are you?" They knew it was the Lord. Jesus came, took
> the bread and gave it to them, and did the same with the fish.

The high priest would have a rope tied around his ankle in case he would make a mistake in the Holy of Holies. This way he could be pulled out of there if God had killed him. Jesus performed the service perfectly so he cooked a feast with his friends to celebrate, and fulfill the law.

Let's look at one more requirement in Yom Kippur before we move onto the Feast of Tabernacles.

> Yoma 8:2
> "One who eats the volume of a large date—like it and its pit— or
> who drinks (the volume of) both his full cheek is liable. (For punishment). All foods combine for the volume of a date, and all
> drinks combine for the volume of his cheekfuls, but food and drink
> do not combine."

Jesus, while he was on the cross, did have one small drink, but it wasn't enough to make him liable, or to break the law.

> John 19:28-30
> Later, knowing that all was now completed, and so that the
> Scripture would be fulfilled, Jesus said, "I am thirsty." A jar of

wine vinegar was there, so they soaked a sponge in it, put the sponge on a stalk of the hyssop plant, and lifted it to Jesus' lips. When he had received the drink, Jesus said, "It is finished." With that, he bowed his head and gave up his spirit.

We see that it took several days for Jesus to fulfill the requirements of Yom Kippur. Normally Yom Kippur is a one-day feast that is held on the tenth day of the month of Tishri. If we look at appendix A, we see that Jesus fulfilled Yom Kippur on God's Time Frame. Remember, "A day is as a thousand years; a thousand years is as a day." So Jesus had one thousand years to fulfill the feast and he did so in the proper order.

Jesus was on earth during the tenth day of creation. Since the calendar on earth is a picture of the calendar in heaven, the tenth day of creation would be the tenth day of the first month, Tishri. So Jesus fulfilled Yom Kippur on God's Time Frame.

The Feast of Tabernacles

Going camping for forty years—my back is getting sore just thinking about this. Don't get me wrong. I love to go camping, just leave my sister at home. Anytime she goes camping with me, it is a disaster. Camping with her in Yosemite National Park one fall was a weekend to remember.

It was nice when we arrived on Friday night, but then things started to change. It got colder and colder, and the rain wouldn't stop. The tent got flooded so we had to sleep in the truck the second night. It never stopped raining except for when the rain turned to snow. After one foot of snow we left for home.

One more camping story. We went to Lake Havasu, Arizona to go camping, where there is always nice weather. Guess what? I have been there fifty times camping and no problem. But never again with my sister. There must have been eighty mile an hour winds. She was sleeping in the truck. I was in the tent. I thought I was going to blow away. I moved all the camping gear into the tent and tried to sleep spread-eagled to hold the tent down. I thought a few times that I was going to blow into the lake. The wind never stopped the whole weekend. I am convinced that if my sister had been with Israel in the desert for those forty years, they would all have died.

The Feast of Tabernacles, or booths, is to remind the Israelites of their wanderings in the desert of Sinai. For forty years the people of Israel had to live in temporary shelters while they traveled in the wilderness.

For one week, the fifteenth through the twenty-second in the Hebrew month of Tishri, temporary dwellings are constructed and lived in by the Israeli people. God lived and walked among the Israeli people while they crossed the desert of Sinai during their exodus from Egypt.

Could this be a picture of future events? The Feast of Tabernacles has not yet been fulfilled on God's Time Frame. This could be a picture of men and women who survive the tribulation period on earth, and have to live in temporary dwellings.

This could also be a picture of men living in temporary dwellings, our bodies, until we receive our heavenly bodies. We are not going to look in depth at this issue here. The following Scripture is a picture of this topic.

> I Corinthians 15:42-55
>
> *So will it be with the resurrection of the dead. The body that is sown is perishable, it is raised imperishable; it is sown in dishonor, it is raised in glory; it is sown in weakness, it is raised in power; it is sown a natural body, it is raised a spiritual body.*
>
> *If there is a natural body, there is also a spiritual body. So it is written: "The first man Adam, a life giving spirit. The spiritual did not come first, but the natural, and after that the spiritual. The first man was of the dust of the earth, the second man from heaven. As was the earthly man, so are those who are of the earth; and as is the man from heaven. And just as we have borne the likeness of the earthly man, so shall we bear the likeness of the man from heaven.*
>
> *I declare to you brothers, that flesh and blood cannot inherit the kingdom of God, nor does the perishable inherit the imperishable. Listen, I tell you a mystery: We will not all sleep but we will be changed—in a flash, in the twinkling of an eye, at the last trumpet. For the trumpet will sound, the dead will be raised*

imperishable, and we will be changed. For the perishable must clothe itself with the imperishable, and the mortal with immortality. When the perishable has been clothed with the imperishable, and the mortal with immortality, then the saying that is written will come true: "Death has been swallowed up in victory."

"Where O Death, is your victory? Where O Death is your sting?"

The focus of the earthly feasts point toward the next major feast or event, on God's Time Frame. The next major feast is the Feast of Tabernacles. The next major event is the Wedding. When Jesus was here on earth, all the feasts and activities pointed toward the Day of Atonement, on God's Time Frame.

Jesus fulfilled Passover, the Feast of Unleavened Bread, the Feast of Firstfruits, and Pentecost on the way to fulfilling, the Day of Atonement on God's Time Frame. Jesus must complete the fall feasts, on man's time frame, to point to the Feast of Tabernacles on God's Time Frame.

Some of the major topics of the Feast of Tabernacles are: the coming kingdom of God, the birth of the Messiah, the dedication of the temple, the outpouring of living water, and the protection of Israel in the wilderness.

This festival occurs on the fifteenth to twenty-first of the Hebrew month of Tishri. The twenty-second of Tishri is called the eighth day (Shemini Azeret). A closing assembly is held for the Feast of Tabernacles on this day.

Jesus was born on Tishri 15, the first day of the Feast of Tabernacles. How do we know this?

> **Luke 2:21**
> *On the eighth day, when it was time to circumcise him, he was named Jesus, the name the angel had given him, before he had been conceived.*

Hebrew law says that all children must be circumcised on the eighth day after their birth. God had a special day set aside for His Son.

> **Genesis 17:12**
> *For the generations to come every male among you who is eight days old must be circumcised including those born in your household or bought with money from a foreigner those who are not your offspring.*

Jesus was not from Joseph, but from God. Let's look at some of the other evidence of Jesus' birth.

Jesus was born in a succah-like structure. Succahs are temporary dwellings that are now constructed for the Feast of Tabernacles.

> **Genesis 33:16-17**
> *So that day Esau started on his way back to Seir, Jacob, however, went to Succoth, where he built a place for himself and made shelters for his livestock, that is why this place is called Succoth.*

Jesus was born in a succah, a dwelling made for livestock, a temporary dwelling still commemorated today during the Feast of Tabernacles.

There are laws on the construction of these dwellings. Through these laws, we can get an idea of what the place was like where Jesus was born. These were the type of dwellings that were used when the Israelites crossed the Sinai, during the exodus. These dwellings will also be used by a war-torn people in the future. We currently see refugees of war-torn countries using succah-like structures as they flee the war.

A Succah

Jesus was born in a succah. Many people believe that Jesus was born in a cave, but this is not true. He was born in a succah. A succah is something like a three-sided shed, made with lattice. Light must be able to shine though the succah for it to be a valid one.

> **Succos 1:1**
> *"A succah must be at least 10 hand breaths high and not more than twenty cubits high."*

Handbreadths are anywhere between 3.2 inches and 3.8 inches. Cubits are 18.9 inches to 22.8 inches.

A succah must have three walls, and there must be at least as much sunlight as shade or it is not a valid succah. The people must sleep in these shelters and eat there during the feast.

The modern-day purpose of staying in these succahs is to slow down one's life and to look at God's creation. Everyone decorates the succah in different ways to fit their personality. Some are more complex than others. When the feast is over, the succah is torn down. A new succah is to be built each year for the feast.

The Light of the World

Jesus is the light of the world! The Feast of Tabernacles points to the coming of the Lord and his power filling the temple. It is a time of great rejoicing.

> Succos 5:1b
> *"Whoever did not see the rejoicing of the first day of Succos never saw rejoicing in his life time. Men with torches would sing and dance, and praise the Lord. Harps, lyres, cymbals, trumpets and other instruments would play. This is a time of great rejoicing."*

> Luke 2:8-20
> *And there were shepherds living out in the fields nearby, keeping watch over their flocks at night. An angel of the Lord appeared to them, and the glory of the Lord shone around them, and they were terrified. But the angel said to them, "Do not be afraid. I bring you good news of great joy that will be for all the people. Today in the town of David a savior has been born to you; he is Christ the Lord. This will be a sign to you: You will find a baby wrapped in cloths and lying in a manger."*
> *Suddenly a great company of the heavenly host appeared with the angel, praising God And saying, "Glory to God in the highest, and on earth peace to men, on whom his favor rests."*

> *When the angels had left them and gone into heaven, the shepherds said to one another, "Let's go to Bethlehem and see this thing that has happened, which the Lord has told us about."*
>
> *So they hurried off and found Mary and Joseph and the baby, who was lying in the manger. When they had seen him, they spread the word concerning what had been told them about this child and all who heard it were amazed at what the shepherds said to them. But Mary treasured up all these things in her heart. The shepherds returned, glorifying and praising God for all the things they had heard and seen, which were just as they had been told.*

The angels in heaven rejoiced over the birth of Jesus, but most of the Jews missed it.

There were four huge candelabra at the temple in the court of the women during this feast. These candelabra had four golden bowls on top them and four ladders went up to each one. Youths carrying pitchers of oil would keep the bowls full.

From worn-out priestly undergarments(swaddling cloths), wicks would be made for the candelabras. Jesus was wrapped in the same cloths just after he was born. These burning candelabra were called the light of the world. Every courtyard in Jerusalem would be lit up from their light.

> John 8:12
> *When Jesus spoke again to the people he said: "I am the light of the world, who ever follows me will never walk in darkness, but will have the light of life."*

Normally, each of the twenty-four priestly divisions would work two weeks a year at the temple. On the major feasts, all of the priestly divisions must work. In addition each division would work for at least three weeks at the pilgrimage feasts. Luke 1:8 shows one of these divisions.

Luke 1:8-9
Once when Zechariah's division was on duty and he was serving as priest before God, He was chosen by lot, according to the custom of the priesthood, to go into the temple of the Lord to burn incense.

I Chronicles 24:1-18 shows the priestly divisions from the tribe of Levi, the ones appointed to serve before the Lord.

This festival shows the time God will rule over the world.

Zechariah 14:9
The Lord will be king over the whole earth. On that day there will be one Lord, and His name is the only name.

Zechariah 14:16-19
Then the survivors from all the nations that have attacked Jerusalem will go up year after year to worship the King, the Lord Almighty, and to celebrate the Feast of Tabernacles. If any of the peoples of the earth do not go up to Jerusalem to worship the King, the Lord Almighty, they will have no rain. If the Egyptian people do not go up and take part, they will have no rain. The Lord will bring on them the plague he inflicts on the nations that do not go up to the Feast of Tabernacles. This will be the punishment of all the nations that do not go up to celebrate the Feast of Tabernacles.

Revelation 21:1-4
Then I saw a new heaven and a new earth, for the first heaven and the first earth had passed away, and there was no longer any sea. I saw the Holy City, the new Jerusalem coming down out of heaven from God, prepared as a bride beautifully dressed for her husband. And I heard a loud voice from the throne saying, Now the dwelling of God is with men, and he will live with them. They will be his people, and God himself will be with them and be their God. He will wipe away every tear from their eyes. There will be no more death or mourning or crying or pain, for the old order of things has passed away.

Seventy bulls are offered up to represent the seventy nations that came from Israel. Numbers 29:2-34 contains the Scripture for the seventy nations. You can study it if you like, but it is too long to key it in here.

Day number one, thirteen bulls are offered up to God. Day number two, twelve bulls are offered up, and so on until day seven of the Feast of Tabernacles, the last day of the feast. Then only seven bulls are offered up to God. The total number of bulls offered up is seventy.

Day One	Day Two	Day Three	Day Four	Day Five	Day Six	Day Seven	Total
13 =	12 =	11 =	10 =	9 =	8 =	7 =	70

The silver and gold vessels used to catch the blood of the sacrifices were passed from one priest to another so quickly that the vessels would look like lightning passing through the temple. This was due to the reflected light from the candelabra and shows a picture of the power of God moving in the temple.

The House of the Water Pouring

One of the major ceremonies is known as "the house of the water pouring." This ceremony happens daily during the feast. A group of priests set about slaughtering the sacrifices. A second group of priests go out the Eastern Gate to the Valley of Motza. The priests cut down willow trees at least twenty-five feet in length, take these willow branches, and stand shoulder, to shoulder thirty feet apart. After a signal they step forward, swinging the willow branches from left to right as they march all the way to the temple. The swinging motion produces the sound of the mighty rushing wind approaching the temple.

At the same time the high priest and his assistant go to the Pool of Siloam to retrieve a vase of living water. The water is placed in a golden vessel and the assistant holds a silver vase of wine. Both sets of priests return to the temple. A shofar is blown and then a flute. The priests with the sacrifices ascend to the altar, placing the sacrifices in the fire. The priests with the willows circle the altar seven times, then lay their willows against the base of the altar, forming a succah (a temporary dwelling for livestock). The high priest and his assistant ascend the altar and pour out the water and the wine. This ceremony shows the time when the power of God will fill the temple as he returns to rule and reign.

> Isaiah 12:3
> With joy you will draw water from the wells of salvation.

> John 7:37-38
> On the last and greatest day of the feast, Jesus stood and said in a loud voice, " if anyone is thirsty, let him come to me and drink. Whoever believes in me, as the Scripture has said, 'streams of living water will flow from within him.'"

The woman caught in adultery would have occurred during the last day of this feast.

> John 8:1-11
> But Jesus went to the Mount of Olives. At dawn he appeared again at the temple courts, where all the people gathered around him, and he sat down to teach them. The teachers of the law and the pharisees brought in a woman caught in adultery. They made her stand before the group and said to Jesus, "Teacher, this woman was caught in the act of adultery. In the Law Moses commanded us to stone such women. Now what do you say?" They were using this question as a trap, in order to have a basis for accusing him. But Jesus bends down and started to write on the ground with his finger. When they kept on questioning him, he straightened up said to them, "If any one of you is without sin, let him be the first to throw a stone at her." Again he stooped down to write on the ground. At this, those who heard began to go away one at a time, the older ones first until only Jesus was left, with the woman still standing there. Jesus straightened up and asked her, "Woman where are they? Has no one condemned you?" "No one, sir," she said. "Then neither do I condemn you," Jesus declared. "Go now and leave your Life of sin."

Jeremiah 17:12-13 tells us what Jesus was writing in the earth.

A glorious throne, exalted from the beginning, is the place of our sanctuary. O Lord the hope of Israel, all who forsake you will be put to shame. Those who turn away from you will be written in the dust because they have forsaken the Lord, the spring of living water.

The Four Species

The four species are different types of fruits and plants that are used during the Feast of Tabernacles. These items are used throughout the whole week of the feast, to help show the power of God.

> Leviticus 23:40
> *On the first day you are to take choice fruit from the trees, and palm fronds, leafy branches and poplars, and rejoice before the Lord your God for seven days.*

The first of the four species is an *esrog*, tasty fruit with a pleasant aroma. This fruit represents righteous people who possess Torah knowledge and good deeds. The *lulav* produces sweet fruit but has no fragrances. This represents a scholar who is proficient in the Torah without good deeds. The myrtle is a person who produces good deeds without Torah knowledge, no fruit but sweet smelling. The last tree is the willow, a person without good deeds or Torah knowledge, an odorless and tasteless tree.

The *lulav* is waved after receiving the blessing over the four species and the reading of Psalms 113-118. The *lulav* is waved in all six directions, south, north, east, up, down, and west. This waving is to represent the people of Israel rejoicing with the trees of the forest. The date palm branches were beaten on the ground around the altar. On the seventh day of the feast, the *esrog* or citron could be eaten by the children.

King Solomon dedicated the temple on the Feast of Tabernacles. We can find this event in 1 Kings.

> I Kings 8:22-24
> *Then Solomon stood before the altar of the Lord in front of the whole assembly of Israel, spread out his hands toward heaven*

and said: " O Lord, God of Israel, there is no God like you in heaven above or on earth below you who keep your covenant of love with your servants who continue wholeheartedly in your way. You have kept your promise to your servant David my father; with your mouth you have promised and with your hand you have fulfilled it as it is today.

Let's skip ahead to verse 65 of I Kings.

I Kings 8:65
So Solomon observed the festival at that time, and all Israel with him—a vast assembly people from Lebo Hamath to the Wadi of Egypt. They celebrated it before the Lord our God for seven days and seven days more, fourteen days in all.

One of the prayers in Luke 2:13-14 is actually found in I Kings.

Luke 2:13-14
Suddenly a great company of the heavenly host appeared with the angel, praising God and saying, "Glory to God in the highest and on Earth peace to men, on who God's favor rests."

An interesting fact about the Feast of Tabernacles was written by Josephus, a secular writer around the first century. A report was written on Alexander Januaeus, a high priest that was considered corrupt and not God's choice as high priest. This man was pelted by the Israelites at the festival with their citrons. At this time the high priesthood was bought by the highest bidder, once every six months, so that the high priest could raid the temple treasury. He closed the temple mount and had six thousand people killed, as he was also king at the time.

We can't go into the detail on the Feast of Tabernacles that we did on the other feasts.

God has not yet fulfilled this feast on his time frame. Later on we will look at trying to piece together part of the border around this puzzle. Once the border is in place, we will be able to look in more detail at the prophecies in the Bible.

OTHER FEASTS

Chanukah

The Festival of Lights. Chanukah starts on the twenty-fifth of the Hebrew month of Kislev, usually in our month of December. Chanukah is some times called "second Succos's" or "the Second Feast of Tabernacles." This feast runs for eight days, just like the Feast of Tabernacles.

The feast celebrates the victory over Antiochus Epiphanes, who desecrated the temple mount in Jerusalem and erected a pagan altar, the abomination of desolation, in 167 B.C. Antiochus prohibited Judaism for several years, and terrible crimes were carried out against the Hebrew people. The people had to deny their God or they would be tortured or killed.

A Hebrew man named Mattathias and his sons rebelled against the Syrian rule and fought for religious freedom in Israel. The Maccabees

(Mattathias and his sons) recaptured the temple mount after defeating the Syrians in 164 B.C.

The temple oil was running low due to the battle with the Syrians. This oil was used in the daily temple services to keep the lamps lit before the Lord. There was only enough oil left to light the temple lamps for one day, but somehow the oil lasted for eight days. This was enough time so that more oil could be made to burn in the menorah. The oil was special and could only be blended for the temple services. If it was used for personal use, the person could be killed by God.

Chanukah means "dedication." The temple was rededicated after the Maccabeanian victory over the Syrians. This feast is also called the Festival of Lights—eight candles are lit during the feast, one for each day the oil miraculously burned.

Jesus was to have been conceived on this festival. If the priestly order is studied around the birth of Jesus, there is a possibility that he was conceived on this date, Kislev 25.

Chanukah is not one of the feasts on God's Time Frame. This means that there will not be a one-thousand-year emphasis on this feast. This is a winter feast and is not considered one of the major fall feasts. The new Jerusalem would have already come down from heaven to earth in the "thousand years are as one day" time frame, before this feast would be celebrated on God's Time Frame. In the future this feast must then take place on man's time frame. There are several references to Chanukah in the Bible, even though it is never mentioned by name.

> Daniel 12:11-12
> *From the time that the daily sacrifice is abolished and the abomination that causes desolation is set up. There will be 1290 days. Blessed is the one who waits for and reaches the end of the 1335 days.*

> Revelation 11:1-3
> *I was given a reed like a measuring rod and was told, go and measure the temple of God and the altar, and count the worshipers there, but exclude the outer court; do not measure it, because it has been given to the gentiles. They will trample on the holy city*

for 42 months, and I will give power to my two witnesses, and they will prophesy for 1260 days' clothed in sackcloth . . .

These references are to the end times and tribulation period. Before we look closer at the above Scriptures we need to review. We have said before that believers in Jesus will be called away on the first of the month of Tishri, the Feast of Trumpets. On this same day the temple sacrifices will be restarted.

I Corinthians 15:51-55
I declare to you, brothers, that flesh and blood cannot inherit the kingdom of God, nor does the perishable inherit the imperishable. Listen, I tell you a mystery: we will not all sleep, but we will all be changed, in a flash, in the twinkling of an eye, at the last trumpet. For the trumpet will sound, the dead will be raised imperishable, and we will be changed, for the perishable must clothe itself with the imperishable, and the mortal with immortality. When the perishable, has been clothed with the imperishable, and the mortal with immortality, then the saying that is written will come true: Death has been swallowed up in victory, "Where, O death, is your victory? Where, O death, is your sting."

Ezra 3:6
On the first day of the seventh month they began to offer burnt offerings to the Lord, though the foundation of the Lord's temple had not yet been laid.

Here again we see the Feast of Trumpets. This is also a picture of the third temple being prepared for construction.

Let's go back now and see how Chanukah fits into the Bible, even though it is never mentioned by name.

Daniel 9:24-28
Seventy "sevens" are decreed for your people and your holy city to finish transgression to put an end to sin, to atone for wickedness

to bring in everlasting righteousness, to seal up visions and prophecy and to anoint the most holy.

Know and understand this: From the issuing of the decree to restore and rebuild Jerusalem until the anointed one, the ruler, comes, there will be rebuilt with streets and a trench, but in times of trouble. After the sixty-two sevens, "The anointed one will be cut off and have nothing. The people of the ruler who will come will destroy the city and the sanctuary. The end will come like a flood: War will continue until the end and desolations have been decreed. He will confirm a covenant with many for one seven. In the middle of the seven he will put an end to sacrifice and offering. And on a wing of the temple, he will set up an abomination that causes desolation, until the end that is decreed is poured out on him.

The sixty-two weeks and the seven weeks are understood to be sixty-nine seven-year periods from the time the decree is issued to rebuild the temple until the temple is to be destroyed again. After the sixty-two weeks Jesus is cut off.

The decree of Artaxerxes to Nehemiah in 444 B.C. seems to fit the prophecy given to Daniel.

> Nehemiah 2:1-8
> In the month of Nisan in the twentieth year of King Artaxerxes, when wine and was brought for him, I took the wine and gave it to the king. I had not been sad in his presence before; so the king asked me, "why does your face look so sad when you are not ill? This can be nothing but sadness of heart.
> I was very much afraid, but I said to the king, "May the king live forever! Why should my face not look sad when the city where my fathers are buried lies in ruins, and its gates have been destroyed by fire?"
> The King said to me, " What is it you want?" Then I prayed to the God of heaven, and I answered the king, "If it pleases the king and if your servant has found favor in his sight, let him send me to the city in Judah where my fathers are buried so that I can rebuild it."

> Then the king, with the queen sitting beside him, asked me, "How long will your journey take, and when will you get back?" It pleased the king to send me; so I set a time.
>
> I also said to him, " If it pleases the king, may I have letters to the governors of Trans-Euphrates, so that they will provide me safe-conduct until I arrive in Judah? And may I have a letter to Asaph, keeper of the king's forest, so he will give me timber to make beams for the gates of the citadel by the temple and for the city wall and for the residence I will occupy?" And because the gracious hand of my God was upon me, the king granted my requests.

Artaxerxes' decree was issued around the first of Nisan 444 B.C. Using the 360-day year times sixty-nine sevens, we get a date when the Messiah is to be cut off. Using the total from the above calculation compared to a 365-day year, we can come up with a date that Jesus arrives in Jerusalem, Nisan 10 on the Hebrew calendar. The day the Lord comes in the city is the day he was to be cut off.

There is still one week left in Daniel's prophecy that needs to be fulfilled. This one week could be part of the "thousand years are as one day" part of God's plan. Seven one-thousand year periods could take mankind from Adam to the thousand-year reign of Christ. But, I believe this Scripture is used on the normal time period as well.

The believers are caught away on the first of the month of Tishri, on the Day of Atonement. Nine days later, the tribulation period starts. A treaty is signed on this day with the Antichrist, and the first three and one-half years of the tribulation period begins. The two Scriptures we looked at earlier, Daniel 12:11-12 and Revelation 11:1-3, are about the second half of the tribulation period.

If we work backwards from the Day of Atonement as the ending of the seven years, we go back to the Feast of Purim, when the abomination that causes desolation is set up in the temple.

When we work backwards from the first day of Chanukah, 1335 days, we come back to Nisan 10. This is the same day Jesus rode into the city before his death and resurrection. So if a believer makes it to Chanukah during the tribulation period, he has made it through the hardest time the earth will ever know.

Purim

The feast of Purim occurs on the fourteenth and fifteenth of the Hebrew month of Adar. This is a time of eating drinking and being merry, as well as giving gifts to the poor.

The book of Esther is read on this feast, to celebrate the victory of the Hebrew people over Haman and his evil counter parts. This event took place during the Babylon captivity of the Hebrew people around the year 400 B.C. I believe Esther is a picture of the bride of Christ, who through her bravery overcomes the wicked Haman, a picture of Satan. Haman and his family are direct decedents of Amalek. The Lord wanted Saul to completely destroy the Amalekites, but Saul was rejected as king by the Lord after this incident:

The Amalekites were destroyed in I Samuel 15:3.

> I Samuel 15:3
> Now go, attack the Amalekites and totally destroy everything that belongs to them. Do not spare them; Put to death men and women, children and infants, cattle and sheep, camels and donkeys.

Saul didn't completely destroy the Amalekites like God asked him to do.

> I Samuel 15:20-23
> But I did obey the Lord, Saul said. "I went on the mission the Lord assigned me.
> I completely destroyed the Amalekites and brought back Agag their king. The soldiers took sheep and cattle from the plunder, the best of what was devoted to God, in order to sacrifice them to the Lord your God at Gilgal."
> Does the Lord delight in burnt offerings and sacrifices as much as in obeying the voice of the Lord? To obey is better than sacrifice, and to heed is better than the fat of rams.
> For rebellion is like the sin of divination, and arrogance like the evil of idolatry. Because you have rejected the word of the Lord, he has rejected you as king.

The Megillah or scroll of Esther is read on Purim. The entire scroll is read, while the people cheer every time the name of Mordecai is read and boo every time the name of Haman is read. The people are to cheer until they don't know the difference between Haman and Mordecai.

There are many pictures or prophecies in the book of Esther, the only book of the Bible where the name of God is not mentioned. Hatikva Ministries has an excellent book on the prophecies in the book of Esther.

We have finished looking at the feasts of Israel. The fasts carry the same in-depth look at the Lord and his people as do the feasts. We will not look at the fasts in this study. The purpose of looking at the feasts was to understand God's appointed times, and to explore the use of these times on the "one thousand years is as one day" time frame. Then we can apply these events to the major events in God's Time Frame. We will be using appendix A and B more in the upcoming part of this study.

A THOUSAND YEARS ARE AS ONE DAY

Biblical Account

Scientists argue that the earth is much older than the biblical account. There is a theory that a large amount of time exists between the first days of creation and our current time. Using the biblical account we can determine that the creation event was approximately eleven thousand years ago. Using the Hebrew calendar, along with the biblical account and God's *mo'ed*, or appointed times, we can see our location in God's plan for this age.

The key for me to unlocking the calendar is the chart in appendix B from the Art Scroll Tannic series on Genesis, an excellent publication on Genesis.

Backtracking from the time of Jacob, you can overlap certain birth days through to the time of the flood, to the creation of Adam and Eve. The Hebrew people believe Eve was created thirteen years after Adam.

Using the Hebrew calendar rather than our own Julian calendar makes our date conversions much easier. There are no years to skip, and no counting backwards, like you do when you convert to B.C. from A.D. We will look more at using date conversions when we try to determine Adam's year of creation, later on in the chapter.

We are currently in year 5,761 in the Hebrew calendar, which translates to 2,001 on today's calendar. Year 5,761 is supposed to be 5,761 years from the creation of Adam. We can track history all the way back to Jacob, but it is difficult to track before the flood. We can see by using appendix B that Noah knew people, or relatives, that knew Adam. This information could have been passed to this side of the flood from another source other than just from God to Moses. God doesn't lie, but Noah and his family could still have been a source of pre-flood information.

The Puzzle Border

Now we are going to show how we came to the conclusions that were developed in appendix A, and how to use these conclusions to show the signs of the times.

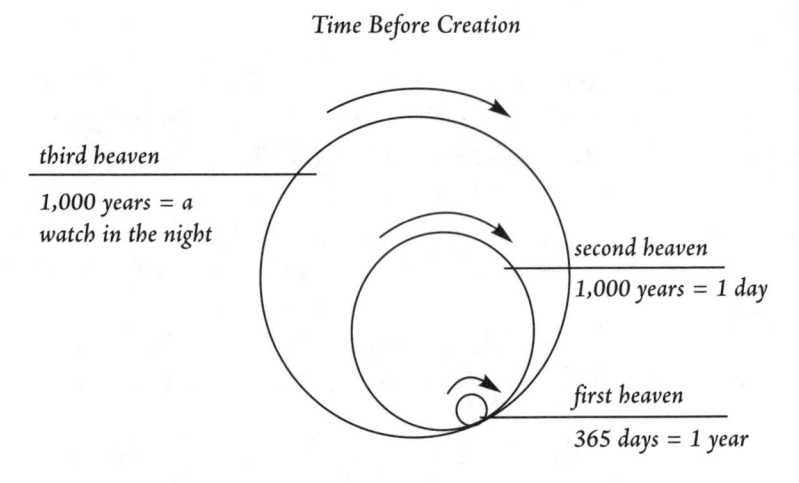

Time Before Creation

third heaven
1,000 years = a watch in the night

second heaven
1,000 years = 1 day

first heaven
365 days = 1 year

The four time frames that are mentioned in the Bible.

The First Day

The first day of creation is Rosh HaShanah, the first day of the month of Tishri, on God's Time Frame. Each following day is the next day of the month of Tishri. Example: The fourth day is the fourth of Tishri, on the "day is as a thousand year's" calendar.

> **Genesis 1:1-5**
> *In the beginning God created the heavens and the earth. Now the earth was formless and empty, darkness was over the surface of the deep, and the spirit of God was hovering over the waters.*
> *And God said, "Let there be light," and there was light. God saw that the light was good, and he separated the light from the darkness. God called the light, "day" and the darkness he called, "night." And there was evening and there was morning the first day.*

Using our study we can determine several unmentioned items in this passage, the first item being that God was outside our time frame in verses 1-5 of Genesis 1. The time frame that God was in at this stage of creation could be the "thousand years are as a watch in the night" that we talked about in Psalm 90:4.

> **Psalms 90:4**
> *For a thousand years in your sight are like a day that has just gone by, or like a watch in the night.*

> **2 Corinthians 12:2**
> *I know a man in Christ who fourteen years ago was caught up to the third heaven. Whether it was in the body or out of the body I do not know God knows.*

Paul shows us that there is a third heaven and possibly a third time frame. The third heaven could be the place where we saw God hovering over the waters in Genesis, before the second plane of time is started, but I believe he was in a fourth time frame, unlimited time.

There is evidence that the three levels of time—365 days equal one year, one thousand years are as a day, and a thousand years are as a watch in the night—all have the same starting point. We know that God is not subject to time as we know it, so he must have been in a fourth level of time. Under day twelve we will look more at the "thousand years are as a watch in the night" theory.

Genesis 1:1-2
In the beginning, God created the heavens and the earth. Now the earth was formless and empty, darkness was over the surface of the deep, and the spirit of God was hovering over the waters.

2 Peter 3:8
But do not forget this one thing, dear friends: With the Lord a day is like a thousand years, and a thousand years are like a day.

For us a thousand years are like one day with the Lord. Using these Scriptures, we know that the first day of creation is one thousand years old. We also know that the day starts at sundown and ends at sundown like the Hebrew day.

When time started in Genesis 1:1-5, this had to have been the first day on the "thousand years are as one day" time frame. This very first day had to be New Years, because there was no time on this plane before the creation event. Using God's *mo'ed* or appointed times we know New Year's is the Feast of Trumpets; the feast of no man knows the day or the hour. The name of this feast seems to fit in this case.

God rests six days later in Genesis 2:1-3. Using this day, we can back up until the first day and see that the earth was created on a Sunday. We also know that the Feast of Trumpets is a high Sabbath, a day of rest. I believe God started the creation event, then rested until this phase of the creation event was completed.

The Second Day

The second day, Monday, is the second day of the Feast of Trumpets and God separated the waters.

Genesis 1:6-8
And God said, "Let there be an expanse between the waters to separate water from water." so God made the expanse and separated the water under the expanse from the water above it. And it was so. God called the expanse "sky." and there was evening and there was morning the second day.

The Third Day

The third day God creates dry ground and starts vegetation. The vegetation is given the ability to reproduce. This is Tuesday on the "thousand years is as one day" calendar. The earth is now between two thousand and three thousand years old. We are still in the days of awe, the time period between the Feast of Trumpets and the Day of Atonement.

Genesis 1:9-13
And God said, "Let the water under the sky be gathered to one place, and let dry ground appear." And it was so. God called the dry ground "land," and the gathered waters he called "seas." And God saw that it was good.

Then God said, "Let the land produce vegetation: seed-bearing plants and trees on the land that bear fruit with seed in it, according to their various kinds." And it was so. The land produced vegetation: plants bearing seed according to their kinds and trees bearing fruit with seed in it according to their kinds. And God saw that it was good. And there was evening and there was morning the third day.

The Fourth Day

The fourth day of creation, Wednesday, the earth is now between three thousand and four thousand years old. We see the creation of the sun, moon and stars.

Genesis 1:14-19
And God said, "Let there be lights in the expanse of the sky to separate the day from the night, and let them serve as signs to

> mark seasons and days and years, and let them serve as signs to mark seasons and days and years, and let them be lights in the expanse of the sky to give light on earth." And it was so. God made two great lights—the greater one to govern the day and the lesser light to govern the night. He also made the stars. God set them in the expanse of the sky to give light on the earth, to separate light from darkness. And God saw that it was good. And there was evening and there was morning—the fourth day.

The Fifth Day

The fifth day, Thursday, God created all the animals of the sea, and the birds of the air. The earth is now between four thousand and five thousand years old.

> **Genesis 1:20-23**
> And God said, "Let the water teem with living creatures, and let birds fly above the earth across the expanse of the sky." So God created the great creatures of the sea and every living and moving thing with which the water teems, according to their kinds, and every winged bird according to its kind. And God saw them and said, "Be fruitful and increase in number and fill the water in the seas, and let the birds increase on the earth." And there was evening and there was morning the fifth day.

The Sixth Day

The first puzzle corner. On the sixth day, Friday, things get more confusing due to man's creation. Animals and man were created during this thousand year period. Adam was created during this time frame. The earth is somewhere between five thousand and six thousand years old.

> **Genesis 1:24-31**
> And God said, "Let the land produce living creatures according to their kinds; livestock, creatures that move along the ground, and wild animals, each according to its kind." And it was so.

> God made the kinds, the livestock according to their kinds, and all the creatures that move along the ground according to their kinds. And God saw that it was good.
>
> Then God said, "Let us make man in our image, in our likeness, and let them rule over the fish of the sea and the birds of the air, over the livestock, over all the creatures of the earth, and over all the creatures that move along the ground." So God created man in his own image in the image of God he created him; male and female he created them.
>
> God blessed them and said to them, "Be fruitful and increase in number; fill the earth and subdue it. Rule over the fish of the sea and the birds of the air and over every living creature that moves on the ground."
>
> Then God said, " I give you every seed-bearing plant on the face of the whole earth and every tree that has fruit with seed in it. They will be yours for food. And to all the beasts of the earth and all the birds of the air and all the creatures on the ground—everything that has the breath of life in it—I give every green plant for food." And it was so.
>
> God saw all that he had made, and it was very good. And there was evening and there was morning—the sixth day.

As we said before, we can track back using the Hebrew calendar and appendix B to tell the year of Adam's creation. The current year on the Hebrew calender is 5,761. The 5,761 is supposed to be the date from Adam's creation. If we work backwards, we can see that Adam was created around the year 442 in the sixth day of creation. God becomes active again after the Sabbath, at the time of the birth of Noah's son Shem. *Shem* means "name" in Hebrew, and he is a picture of Jesus. The Jewish people believe Shem is Melchizedek.

Shem still had the pre-flood life span after God had reduced man's life span to 120 years or less in Genesis 6:3.

> **Genesis 6:3**
> Then the Lord said, "My spirit will not contend with man forever, for he is mortal; his days will be a hundred and twenty years."

Psalm 90:10A
The length of our days is seventy years or eighty, if we have the strength;

Shem lived to be 600 years old, when a normal man would have lived to be anywhere from 70 to 120 years old. Shem would have outlived many generations of the Hebrew people, giving them the impression that he lived forever.

Shem was born 98 years before the flood and ended a more than one-thousand-year period of inactivity in the Bible for God. The flood was 1656 years after Adam's creation. So if we subtract 98 years from the start of the flood we have the start of the eighth day.

The exception to God's inactivity during the Sabbath is the rapture of Enoch.

God had to work with Noah and prepare the animals and the ark before the great flood. The flood starts near the beginning of the eighth day, if we count backwards using the birth days and the ages of the others mentioned in the Bible, we can see that Adam was created in year 442 of the sixth day. (See appendix B) The sixth day started on year 5,000 because the first day starts at zero.

So if we add the years of the earth's creation before Adam, and the years after, we can see the age of the earth. 1656 year of the flood - 98 years Shem's birth - 2000 years the sixth and seventh day = -442. 442 + 5000 for the fifth day = 5442. Adam was created in the morning of the sixth day, just before sunrise. Remember that the Hebrew day starts in the evening and ends at sunset.

Years from Adams creation	5,761	(Hebrew Calendar)
Adams creation	5,442	(Up to Adam)
Years	11,203	(Age of the earth)

Genesis 2:7
The Lord God formed the man from the dust of the ground and breathed into his nostrils the breath of life, and the man became a living being.

Adam and Eve were tempted by Satan in Genesis 3:6.

> **Genesis 3:6**
> *When the woman saw that the fruit of the tree was good for food and pleasing to the eye, and also desirable for gaining wisdom, she took some and ate it. She also gave some to her husband, who was with her and he ate it.*

Starting now, Revelation 2:10 is in effect.

> **Revelation 2:10**
> *Do not be afraid of what you are about to suffer. I tell you, the devil will put some of you in prison to test you, and you will suffer persecution for ten days. Be faithful, even to the point of death, and I will give you the crown of life.*

In this passage the Lord tells the church of Smyrna they will suffer persecution for ten days. This is where God's *mo'ed*, or appointed times, starts to stand out. If we look at appendix A for the ten thousand years after Adam's creation, we are suddenly put into the Feast of Tabernacles on God's Time Frame. The earth would be about 15,450 years old at this point. The fifteenth of the Hebrew month of Tishri is the first day of the Feast of Tabernacles. Satan would be thrown into the lake of fire on the second day of the feast.

If we look again at the book of Revelation, we see Satan being released on day thirteen of creation. The earth would be about 12,450 years old at the time of his trial. He would be thrown into the lake of fire on the sixteenth day of creation, in the early part of the day. We will look more at how we came up with this date on day thirteen. Just go with it for now.

> **Revelation 20:7-15**
> *When the thousand years are over, Satan will be released from his prison and will go out to deceive the nations in the four corners of the earth—Gog and Magog—to gather them for battle. In number they are like the sand on the seashore. They marched across the breadth of the earth and surrounded the camp of God's people,*

> the city he loves. But fire came down from heaven and devoured them. And the devil, who deceived them, was thrown into the lake of burning sulfur, where the beast and the false prophet had been thrown. They will be tormented day and night forever and ever.
> Then I saw a great white throne and him who was seated on it. Earth and sky fled from his presence, and there was no place for them. And I saw the dead, great and small, standing before the throne, and books were opened. Another book was opened, which is the book of life. The dead were judged according to what he had done. Then death and Hades were thrown into the lake of fire. The lake of fire is the second death. If anyone's name was not found written in the book of life, he was thrown into the lake of fire.

Satan and anyone whose name is not written in the Lamb's Book of Life is thrown into the lake of fire.

> **Revelation 21:1-3**
> Then I saw the new heaven and a new earth, for the first heaven and the first earth had passed away, and there was no longer any sea. I saw the Holy City the new Jerusalem, coming down out of heaven from God, prepared as a bride beautifully dressed for her husband. And I heard a loud voice from the throne saying, "Now the dwelling of God is with men, and he will live with them. They will be his people, and he will be their God."

There is a new heaven and a new earth as God's tabernacle comes down from heaven. Remember the great rejoicing of the Feast of Tabernacles and that Jesus is the light of the world.

We have a picture of the ten days of suffering in Jeremiah. These events in Revelation 2:10 and Jeremiah 42:7-10 seem to be related to each other.

> **Jeremiah 42:7-10**
> Ten days later the word of the Lord came to Jeremiah. So he called together Johanan son of Kareah and all the army officers who were with him and all the people from the least to the greatest. He

> said to them, this is what the Lord, the God of Israel, to whom
> you sent me to present your petition, says: If you stay in this land,
> I will build you up and not tear you down; I will plant you and
> not uproot you, for I am grieved over the disaster I have inflicted
> on you.

There is another picture of the ten days of temptation in I Samuel 25. David is watching over Nabel and his household. Nabel acts with disrespect to David and his men, denying them food for the protection David and his men provided. By the way, *Nabel* means "fool" in Hebrew. Could this be a picture of foolish Satan?

> I Samuel 25:38
> About ten days later the Lord struck Nabel and he died.

David and his men are a picture of men filled with the Holy Spirit. Nabel is a picture of Satan being thrown into the lake of fire ten days from Adam's sin on God's Time Frame of one thousand years as a day. Could Daniel 1:11-14 be another picture of God's people being tested?

> Daniel 1:11-14
> Daniel then said to the guard whom the chief official had
> appointed over Daniel, Hananiah, Mishael, and Azariah,
> "please test your servants for ten days: Give us nothing but veg-
> etables to eat and water to drink. Then compare our appearance
> with that of the young men who eat the royal food, and treat
> your servants in accordance with what you see." So they agreed
> to this and tested them for ten days.

> Acts 25:6
> After spending eight or ten days with them, he went down to
> Caesarea, and the next day, he convened the court and ordered
> that Paul be brought before him.

Why would Paul say eight or ten days? Why not nine or ten or eight or nine days? Ten days on the "thousand years are as one day" calendar takes us from Adam's creation to the Feast of Tabernacles, ten thousand years later, when the new Jerusalem comes down from heaven. Eight days takes us to the thousand-year reign of Jesus Christ. The ninth day is God's Sabbath, on the "thousand years are as one day" time frame. The heavenly court would be off duty on the Sabbath.

Paul is a picture of the people who have been brought before the Lord to be judged. Festus is a picture of the king judging the people. Festus can find no fault with Paul, a picture of God and the church.

That's all we are going to look at on day fifteen of God's calendar and the Feast of Tabernacles at this time.

The Seventh Day

The seventh day is the Sabbath, God's day of rest. We don't see much interaction between God and man recorded in the Bible during this day. There is more than 1000 years in the Bible where God does nohing except rapture Enoch. Enoch was the first person born on this day in the Bible. Chapter five of Genesis and the beginning of chapter six show more than one thousand years of inactivity on God's part—this is His Sabbath. We do see man multiplying on the earth during this time.

> Genesis 2:2-3
> *By the seventh day God had finished the work he had been doing; so on the seventh day he rested from all his work. And God blessed the seventh day and made it holy, because on it he rested from all the work of creating that he had done.*

Evil runs wild through the earth while God is resting.

> Genesis 6:5-8
> *The Lord saw how great man's wickedness on the earth had become, and that every inclination of the thoughts of his heart was evil all the time. The Lord was grieved that he had made man on the earth, and his heart was filled with pain. So the Lord said, I will wipe mankind whom I have created, from the face of the earth men and animals, and creatures that move*

along the ground, and birds of the air—for I am grieved that I have made them.

God is resting and his people are running wild through the earth. God gave us a commandment to keep the Sabbath and make it holy. We know that there is a Sabbath every seven days on God's Time Frame. If we add seven thousand years to the first Sabbath of God, we need to look at the fourteenth day of God's creation. The earth would be around thirteen thousand to fourteen thousand years old.

Let's see what God says about his rest.

Hebrews 4:1-10
Therefore, since the promise of entering his rest still stands, let us be careful that none of you be found to have fallen short of it. For we also have had the gospel preached to us, just as they did; but the message they heard was of no value to them, because those who heard did not combine it with faith. Now we who have believed enter that rest, just as God has said, "So I declared on oath in my anger, they shall never enter my rest." "And yet his work has been finished since the creation of the world. For somewhere he has spoken about the seventh day God rested from his work." And again in the passage above he says, "They will never enter my rest."

It still remains that some will enter that rest, and those who formerly had the gospel preached to them did not go in, because of their disobedience. Therefore God again set a certain day, calling it today, when a long time later spoke through David, as was said before: "Today, if you hear his voice, do not harden your hearts."

For if Joshua had given them rest, God would not have spoken later about another day.

There remains, then a Sabbath-rest for the people of God; for anyone who enters God's rest also rests from his own work, just as God did from his.

We see God's rest on day seven and day fourteen of creation. We also see Enoch entering into God's rest on the seventh day.

> **Genesis 5:21-24**
> *When Enoch had lived 65 years, he became the father of Methuselah, Enoch walked with God 300 years and had other sons and daughters. Together, Enoch lived 365 years. Enoch walked with God; Then he was no more, because God took him away.*

Enoch walked with God and was taken to God's rest; this is a picture of God's church being with him during his Sabbath.

We see the same evil on day seven as we do on day fourteen, as God is resting on those days. Satan is very active.

The Eighth Day

In 2 Chronicles, we see a picture of the Lord consecrating the temple to remove all the unclean items and repairing the temple.

> **2 Chronicles 29:15-17**
> *When they had assembled their brothers and consecrated themselves, they went in to purify the temple of the Lord, as the king had ordered, following the word of the Lord. The priests went into the sanctuary of the Lord to purify it. They brought out to the courtyard of the Lord's temple everything unclean that they found in the temple of the Lord. The Levites took it and carried it out to the Kidron Valley. They began the consecration on the first day of the first month, and by the eighth day of the month they reached the portico of the Lord. For eight more days they consecrated the temple of the Lord itself, finishing on the sixteenth day of the first month.*

The eighth day of creation contains the flood. This is the consecration mentioned in the above passage. We will look more at the flood a little later.

Kidron Valley is a picture of the lake of fire in Jewish legends. Everything that was considered trash or unclean was dumped in the Kidron Valley. This was everything from household garbage to unclaimed dead bodies. A fire was always burning there, just like the lake of fire.

If we jump ahead to day sixteen, this is the day Satan in thrown into the lake of fire. (See day sixteen.) On day sixteen God is mopping up the evil as the new heaven and earth are prepared and the new Jerusalem is made ready. Let's go back to the eighth day.

Noah and his family were brought through the flood by God's hand. I believe the eighth day starts with the birth of Shem, Noah's middle son. Then God closes the door on the ark for Noah and his family. The lifting of the door would be considered work and would not be allowed on the Sabbath. Up until this time Noah and his family did all the physical work of building the ark.

Genesis 7:16b
Then the Lord shut him in.

Genesis 7:6
"Noah was six hundred years old when the flood waters came on the earth."

Genesis 8:15-22
Then God said to Noah, "Come out of the ark, you and your wife and your sons and their wives. Bring out every kind of living creature that is with you—the birds, the animals, and all the creatures that move along the ground—so they can multiply on the earth and be fruitful and increase in number upon it."

So Noah came out, together with his sons and his wife and his son's wives. All the animals and all the creatures that move along the ground and all the birds—everything that moves on the earth—came out of the ark, one kind after another.

Then Noah built an altar to the Lord and, taking some of all the clean animals and clean birds, he sacrificed burnt offerings on it. The Lord smelled the pleasing aroma and said in his heart: never will I curse the ground because of man, even though every inclination of his heart is evil from childhood. And never again will I destroy all living creatures, as I have done. As long as the earth endures, seedtime and harvest, cold and heat, summer and winter, day and night will never cease.

If we jump ahead one week on the "thousand years are as one day" calendar, we are around the fifteenth day, the Feast of Tabernacles, on God's calendar. We see new Jerusalem completed and being prepared to come to earth from heaven. There is great rejoicing in heaven.

Let's look at some of the historical events on day eight of creation. Isaac is born to Abraham and was later used to test him. Isaac was born 1,948 years after Adam was created. Some of the other events on day eight of creation are Israel moving down to Egypt, and Moses later leading the people of Israel to the promised land. The book of Judges takes place during this time.

> Genesis 21:2-3
> *Sarah became pregnant and bore a son to Abraham in his old age, at the very time God had promised him. Abraham gave the name of Isaac to the son Sarah bore him.*

There were many more events on the eighth day of creation. The ones listed here were just enough to show the signs of the times.

The Ninth Day

On the ninth day, we see the time of the kings of Israel, King David, King Solomon, and the other kings of Israel. We see Israel splitting into two kingdoms, around year 2,830 from the creation of Adam. We also see Jerusalem fall to Babylon and the exiles return, seventy years later.

A major portion of the intertestamental period falls here—the time between the last writing of Scripture and the coming of the Lord Jesus. Around two hundred years of the four-hundred-year intertestamental period falls on day nine.

The Tenth Day

The second puzzle corner is the tenth day of creation, the most important day to mankind. It is the tenth day of the Hebrew month of Tishri, on the "thousand years are as a day" calendar. This is the Day of

Atonement, a High Sabbath, and the holiest day of the year. The intertestmental period ends, and Jesus is born about 3,754 years after Adam. Jesus fulfills all the spring feasts, Passover, Unleavened Bread, First Fruits, and Pentecost, on man's time frame, as well as the Day of Atonement on God's Time Frame. We already saw what Jesus did to complete these feasts in earlier chapters. The Holy Spirit is also poured out on this day of creation.

Jerusalem is destroyed by Rome in A.D. 70, year 3,830 from the creation of Adam, and the early Christian movement is in full swing on this day.

> Acts 2:1-4
> When the day of Pentecost came, they were all together in one place. Suddenly a sound like the blowing of a violent wind came from heaven and filled the whole house where they were sitting. They saw what seemed to be tongues of fire that separated and came to rest on each of them. All of them were filled with the Holy Spirit and began to speak in other tongues as the Spirit enabled them.

The Holy Spirit is given to man on this day.

> Judges 11:40
> That each year the young women of Israel go out for four days to commemorate the daughter of Jephthah The Gileadite.

The daughter of Jephthah the Gileadite was sacrificed because her father said He would offer up the first thing that comes out of his home if God would give him the victory in his fight with the Ammonites in Judges 11:29-40.

This could be a picture of Israel from the time of Adam's creation until Jesus curses the fig tree.

> Matthew 21:19-22
> Seeing the fig tree by the road, he went up to it but found nothing on it except leaves. Then he said to it, "may you never bear fruit again!" Immediately the tree withered.

When the disciples saw this, they were amazed. "How did the fig tree wither so quickly?" They asked.

Jesus replied, "I tell you the truth, if you have faith and do not doubt, not only can you do what was done to the fig tree, but you can say to this mountain, 'Go, throw yourself into the sea,' and it will be done. If you believe, you will receive whatever you ask for in prayer."

This withered fig tree is a picture of Jesus' first wife's death—Israel as his first wife that we talked about on the Day of Atonement. As we said before, the Church was to become the bride of the high priest, if the first wife would die for some reason. With the death of the fig tree, we see a picture of the death of Israel and the believers in Jesus as the new bride.

In Genesis chapter 40 (the Scripture is too long to key in here) both servants of Pharaoh had dreams interpreted by Joseph. Both results were to take place three days from Joseph's interpretation. One servant was to be restored to his position and the second servant was to be killed by the king. Both servants are pictures of men—one picture being the people who have accepted Jesus as Lord. The second servant pictures the men who are cast into the lake of fire for not accepting him.

Joshua is God's representative. He replaced Moses after his death as the leader of the Jewish people. Joshua is also a picture of Jesus and we are the people who are going to take possession of the kingdom of God.

Joshua 1:10-11
So Joshua ordered the officers of the people: "Go through the camp and tell the people, 'Get your supplies ready. Three days from now you will cross the Jordan here to go in and take possession of the land the Lord your God is giving you for your own.'"

The Eleventh Day

On the eleventh day of creation, we see the crusades. This time frame covers from around A.D. 800 to the late 1790s. We see mankind exploring the earth and many new inventions during this time period.

The Twelfth Day

The third puzzle corner is the twelfth day of creation. As we said before, Hebrew weddings take place on Thursday evening on the Hebrew calendar, and Wednesday evening on our calendar. I believe we are in the process of being restored to God on this day. When we have been completely restored, we will be raptured. If we look at appendix A, we can see the days of the week.

Revelation 19:7-9
Let us rejoice and be glad and give him glory! For the lamb has come and his bride has made herself ready. Fine linen, bright and clean, was given to her to wear. Then the angel said to me, "Blessed are those who are invited to the wedding supper of the Lamb!" And he added, "These are the words of God."

I Thessalonians 4:16-18
For the Lord himself will come down from heaven, with the loud command, with the voice of the archangel and with the trumpet call of God, and the dead in Christ will rise first.

After that, we who are still alive and are left will be caught up in the clouds to meet the Lord in the air. And so we will be with the Lord forever. Therefore, encourage each other with these words.

The church goes to be with the Lord in the air and a wedding takes place. We are currently in year 5,761 on the Hebrew calendar, 2,001 on our calendar. The Gemara teaches that the world will end after 6,000 years. One of Barnabas' letters states that Jesus will return 6,000 years after Adam's creation. If we add the date of Adam's creation to the 6,000 calendar date, we should be close to the time of Christ's return.

Adam's creation date	5,442
Hebrew calendar date	6,000
Possible date of Jesus return	11,442

If we subtract this date of 11,442 from our current date of 11,203, we could have about two hundred forty years before the return of Jesus. There are other factors or prophecies to help us establish this date.

> **Matthew 24:32-35**
> *Now learn this lesson from the fig tree: As soon as its twigs get tender and its leaves come out, you know that summer is near. Even so, when you see all these things, you know that it is near, right at the door. I tell you the truth, this generation will certainly not pass away until all these things have happened. Heaven and Earth will pass away, but my words will never pass away.*

In the Bible, Israel is always depicted as the fig tree, and a biblical generation is forty years. Israel became a nation in 1948. If we add 40 years to 1948 we get 1988. Israel captured Jerusalem in 1967. If we add 40 years to 1967 we get 2007. There are still other options on this issue. Do the two days between Jesus leaving earth and his return start when he was born, when he died, or when he ascended into heaven? There still could be another option—the year Jerusalem was destroyed. A.D. 70 plus 2000 years could also be the starting point on this issue. Even though we don't know the exact year of the return of Jesus for his Church, we do know that the wedding is in the early part of the Hebrew Thursday, our current Wednesday night on God's Time Frame.

> **Hosea 6:2**
> *After two days he will revive us; on the third day he will restore us; that we may live in his presence.*

The Scripture in Hosea 6:2 takes us into the one-thousand-year reign of Christ. The starting point for the three days is when Jesus was on earth, and this takes us up to the wedding.

Some of the major events of day twelve of creation: Israel becomes a nation in 1948. Israel is born again. We see the Lord's first wife being born again. Leah and Rachel, Jacob's two wives are pictures of Israel and the Church. If you want to read this story in the Bible, Genesis 29:14 through the end of the book of Genesis tells the story of Jacob. Israel is Rachel and the Church is Leah.

> Luke 21:29-33
> He told them this parable: "Look at the fig tree and all the trees. When they spout leaves, you can see for yourselves and know that summer is near. Even so, when you see these things happening, you will know that the kingdom of God is near."
> I tell you the truth, this generation will not pass away until all these things have happened. Heaven and earth will pass away, but my words will never pass away.

Satan is bound and thrown into the pit; the beast and the false prophet are thrown into the lake of fire.

> Revelation 20:1-3
> And I saw an angel coming down out of heaven having the key to the Abyss and holding in his hand a great chain. He seized the dragon, that ancient serpent, who is the devil, and bound him for a thousand years. He threw him into the Abyss, and locked and sealed it over him, to keep him from deceiving the nations anymore until the thousand years were ended. After that, he must be set free for a short time.

> Revelation 19:19-20
> Then I saw the beast and the kings of the earth and their armies gathered together to make war against the rider on the horse and his army. But the beast was captured, and with him the false prophet who had performed the miraculous signs on his behalf. With these signs he had deluded those who had received the mark of the beast and worshiped his image. The two of them were thrown alive into the fiery lake of burning sulfur.

If we look again at the third heaven, where one thousand years is as a watch in the night, one day is equal to six thousand years. Using the same starting point as the first and second heaven, the time frame in the third heaven would fit perfectly if we apply the Hebrew calendar. In day twelve we see the Son turning the kingdom over to the Father, who is one in the same.

We already talked about Rosh HaShanah being a two-day feast. Using the "day is as a watch in the night" theory on the Hebrew calendar, we can see that the Father could be coming off the High Sabbath after day twelve. These two six-thousand-year periods would equal two days on the third heaven's time frame. That would put us in day twelve on the second heaven, or what we are describing as God's Time Frame here in this study. If we apply the fourth grade math problem that we used in the chapter on the Sabbath, we don't have enough of numbers to create a pattern and predict future results from Scripture.

30,1, 2

We only have the first two days of this calendar and the last day of the previous year's calendar. The moon was seen too late in the day to have the first six thousand years be New Year's on the third level of time. Men were created too late in the sixth day, on this level of time, to be a witness to the new moon and two are needed to proclaim the start of the new year. In the third level of time, the first day of the year starts at the beginning of the seventh day on the "thousand years is as a day" calendar. (See the section on Rosh Chodesh.) If this is in fact the third level of time, we have another problem. God says that He is above all things and is not subject to time as we know it. This means that God lives in a fourth time frame because His level of time was not subject to the creation event.

In Revelation 19:6 we see the kingdom being turned over to the Father.

> **Revelation 19:6**
> *Then I heard what sounded like a great multitude, like the roar of rushing waters and like loud peals of thunder, shouting: Hallelujah! For our Lord God Almighty reigns.*

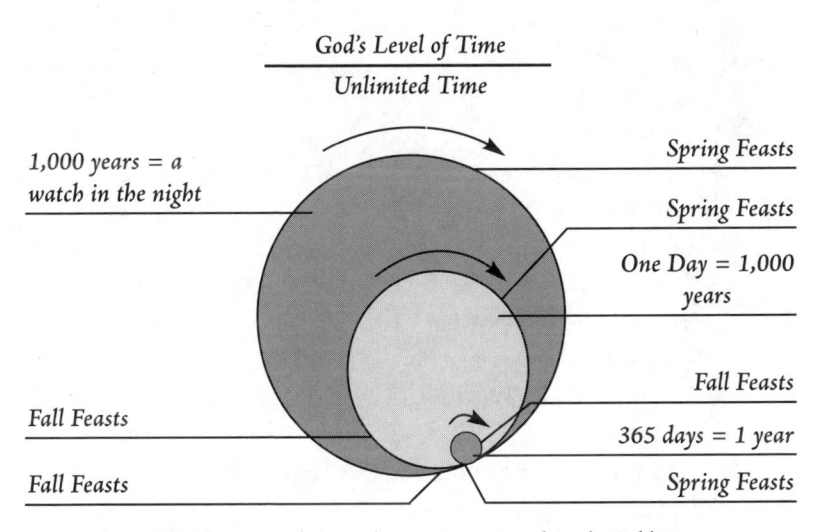

```
                God's Level of Time
                  Unlimited Time

1,000 years = a                    Spring Feasts
watch in the night
                                   Spring Feasts

                                   One Day = 1,000
                                        years


                                    Fall Feasts
Fall Feasts
                                   365 days = 1 year

Fall Feasts                         Spring Feasts
```

The four time frames that are mentioned in the Bible.

The coronation for a new Hebrew king takes place on Rosh HaShanah. One of the names for this feast is the Day of Coronation. Rosh HaShanah, on the second level of time, had already passed before Jesus came to earth as a man. This happened on the first day of the "day is as a thousand years" calendar. His becoming king could not have happened on the current calendar of 365 days equals one year, because he was not proclaimed king in the fall. He was called the coming king at his birth.

Pilate hung a sign above Jesus while he was on the cross that proclaimed Jesus as king of the Jews. Jesus was crucified in the spring, not during the fall feast of Rosh HaShanah. Jesus was on earth during the third level of time, where one thousand years are as a watch in the night. The first two days on this level would mean that Pilate's claim of Jesus being the king of the Jews would be on the second day of the feast of Rosh HaShanah, fulfilling the law.

There is a proper coronation for Jesus in the book of Revelation, and this should also be on the second day of this level of time. This coronation could take place as far as eight hundred years away, and as near as seven years from the time of the signing of the peace treaty between Israel and its neighbors. There are several Scriptures that proclaim Jesus as king: John 1:48-49, Zechariah 9:9, and Luke 19:37-38. Pilate's claim is listed below:

> John 19:19-22
> *Pilate had a notice prepared and fastened to the cross. It read: Jesus of Nazareth, The King of The Jews. Many of the Jews read this sign, for the place where Jesus was crucified was near the city, and the sign was written in Aramaic, Latin, and Greek. The chief priests of the Jews protested to Pilate, "Do not write ' The King of The Jews,' but that this man claimed to be king of the Jews."*
> *Pilate answered, "What I have written, I have written."*

This is a time of great mourning as a large portion of the population is killed due to several large wars in the Middle East. This feast, on the "watch in the night" time frame, ends when the eighteenth day arrives on the second level of time. Sin is completely defeated by the time day eighteen arrives on God's Time Frame.

There is a theory that Jesus fulfilled all things when he was on earth. He was all man, the high priest, the king, and God all at the same

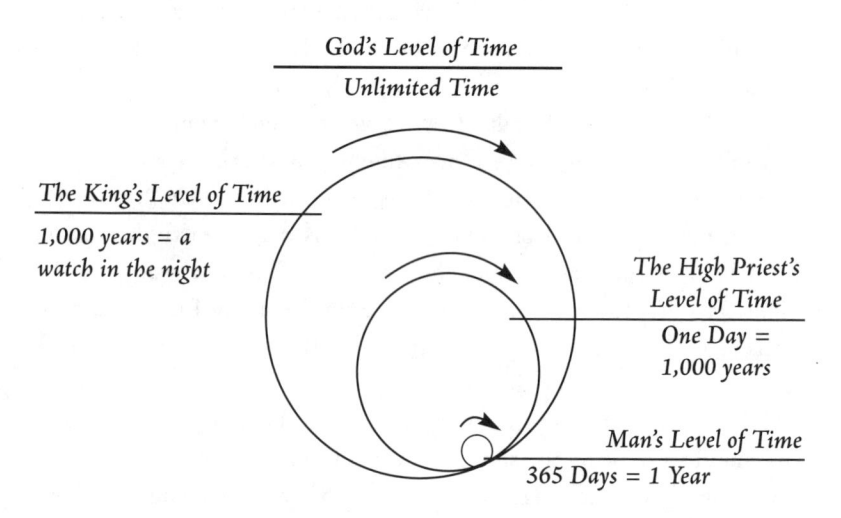

God's Level of Time
Unlimited Time

The King's Level of Time
1,000 years = a watch in the night

The High Priest's Level of Time
One Day = 1,000 years

Man's Level of Time
365 Days = 1 Year

The four time frames that are mentioned in the Bible.

time. The four gospels represent this concept. Mark is supposed to represent Jesus as man on earth. The gospel of Matthew is supposed to represent Jesus as our high priest. The book of Luke is to show Jesus as our king. The book of John shows Jesus as God.

If we look at each of these gospels, we can see that there is one time frame for each one. The gospel of Mark takes place on man's time frame, of one year is equal to 365 days. The gospel of the high priest, Matthew, takes place on the "thousand years are as a day" time frame. Luke, the gospel of the king, takes place on the "day is as a watch in the night" time frame, where a day is as six thousand years. The last time frame, the time frame of God, takes place in a level that is greater than the creation event, because He was before creation. Through the four gospels we can see Jesus working on all four levels at the same time.

God's different levels of time work together like a combination lock. We have a good example of this in day twelve. When we were children, we all had combination locks on our bikes. The locks had three sets of numbers per lever, numbered from one to ten. When the right combination of numbers lined up, the lock would open. If we exchange each number on the lock for one of the Jewish feasts, we can open up day twelve. If we set the first lever to Rosh HaShanah, on the 365 day calendar, and the second lever on the Wedding, on the "thousand years are as a day" calendar, and we set the third lever to Rosh HaShanah on the day is as six thousand years calendar, the lock opens.

The Thirteenth Day

The one question that has always bothered me is how is Jesus going to rule the earth for one thousand years and for all eternity at the same time? Why is the thousand-year reign of Christ going to end? The thousand-year reign of Christ starts during the twelfth day of creation and runs into the thirteenth day. Adam's sin occurred sometime after Eve was created in 5,455, so shortly after year 455 of the sixth day, Adam sinned. At the time there was about fifteen hundred years before the flood. The flood occurs after God comes off his Sabbath.

The same pattern occurs on day thirteen. The thousand-year reign will carry on almost half way through the thirteenth day of creation.

Satan is then let out of the pit for around fifteen hundred years until God's Sabbath ends. There is an additional one thousand years because of the High Sabbath, then the earth is destroyed by fire. Day fourteen is the second Sabbath on God's Time Frame. Day fifteen is the first day of the Feast of Tabernacles.

> Revelation 20:7-8
> *When the thousand years are over, Satan will be released from his prison and will go out to deceive the nations in the four corners of the earth—Gog and Magog—to gather them for battle. In number they are like the sand on the seashore.*

Satan is released from the pit and everyone not written into the Lamb's Book of Life, or the book of the wicked is given another chance to accept Jesus. These are the people who never had the chance to accept Jesus as Savior.

The Fourteenth Day

The earth is now thirteen to fourteen thousand years old. In day fourteen of creation we see God resting, because it is a Sabbath. We talked a lot about the Sabbath under day seven of creation. Please refer to day seven.

The Fifteenth Day

On day fifteen of creation, the earth is fourteen to fifteen thousand years old. This is the Feast of Tabernacles, on the "thousand years are as one day" calendar. All of God's feasts and festivals on man's time frame in day fifteen point to the Feast of Tabernacles on God's Time Frame. There is great rejoicing as the New Jerusalem is prepared to come to earth.

The Sixteenth Day

On the fourth and last puzzle border, evil gets worse on earth, and Gog and Magog come against Israel for a second time.

Revelation 20:9
They marched across the breadth of the earth and surrounded the camp of God's people, the city he loves. But fire came down from heaven and devoured them.

The Great White Throne Judgement starts here and ends in day seventeen. Remember that the daytime hours on this level of time start about 500 years into the day. The first 500 years are the evening hours. Let's look at the book of Revelation.

Revelation 20:11-15
Then I saw a great white throne and him who was seated on it. Earth and sky fled from his presence and there was no place for them. And I saw the dead, great and small, standing before the throne, and the books were opened. Another book was opened, which is the book of life. The dead were judged according to what they had done as recorded in the books. The sea gave up the dead that were in it, and death and Hades gave up the dead that were in them, and each person was judged according to what he has done. Then death and Hades were thrown into the lake of fire. The lake of fire is the second death. If anyone's name is not found written in the book of life, he was thrown into the lake of fire.

This is the day Satan is thrown into the lake of fire, 4,200 years from the year 2000. Unbelievers will be thrown into the lake of fire on both the thirteenth, sixteenth, and seventeenth days of creation. This is the second death.

Zephaniah 1:18
Neither their silver nor their gold will be able to save them on the day of God's wrath. In the fire of his jealousy the whole world will be consumed, for he will make a sudden end of all who live in the earth.

The Seventeenth Day

The earth is sixteen to seventeen thousand years old. The first part of this day is still the White Throne Judgement. The last thing thrown into the lake of fire on this day is death and Hades.

> Revelation 20:15
> *If anyone's name was not found in the book of life, he was thrown into the lake of fire.*

> Deuteronomy 1:2
> *It takes eleven days to go from Horeb to Kadesh Barnea by the Mount Seir road.*

This is the time it takes to go from the mountain of God to defeat the Amalekites and the Ammorites. *Kadesh* means "spring of judgement or justice." The evil on earth is now completely defeated. We are now of one mind with God.

The Eighteenth to Twenty-First Day

> Revelation 21:1-3
> *Then I saw a new heaven and a new earth, for the old heaven and the first earth had passed away, and there was no longer any sea. I saw the Holy City the new Jerusalem coming down out of heaven from God, prepared as a bride beautifully dressed for her husband. And I heard a loud voice from the throne saying, "Now the dwelling of God is with men, and he will live with them. They will be his people, and he will be their God."*

> Matthew 3:15
> *Jesus replied, "Let it be so; it is proper for us to do this to fulfill all righteousness." Then John consented.*

The Twenty-Second Day

We see Jesus at the water pouring ceremony on the Greatest Day of the Feast of Tabernacles, offering the water of life.

Revelation 22:17
The Spirit and the Bride say, "Come!" and let him who hears say, "Come!" Whoever is thirsty, let him come, and whoever wishes, let him take the free gift of the water of life.

WHERE ARE WE NOW?

Jesus fulfilled the feasts on every level of time at the same time while he was with us on earth. So where do we stand on God's Time Frame? What are the coming events that mankind can look toward? To answer these questions, we need to go back to the time of Joshua. Since believers in Christ are about to cross into the promised land, heaven, we need to look at the conquest of a city called Jericho.

What was so special about this city? This was the first city in the promised land that was to be taken by Israel. The people were to follow the ark of God and travel around the city for six days. The people were to remain quiet as they walked around the city, one time on each of the first six days. On the seventh day they were to walk around the city seven times. With a trumpet blast and a shout, the walls of the city would fall down and the people would go straight in and take the city. This story is located in Joshua, chapter six.

As we had said before, six thousand years from the creation of Adam (see day six) puts us into our current time frame. We are near the end of day six. This day could end at any time between now and year A.D. 2240 We have been going around the kingdom of heaven for almost six full days since the creation of Adam. Soon there will be a trumpet blast, a shout from the archangel and we will go in and take the kingdom of heaven. What a great day that will be for believers in the Lord Jesus. Nonbelievers will be left wondering what happened, and unknowingly awaiting the judgement of God in the next several years. People who do not accept Jesus as Lord and Savior will be cast into the lake of fire for all eternity. God's people will live in bliss without temptation from the devil. There will be no more tears.

To accept Jesus as Savior and Lord and be exempt from God's coming tribulation on the earth, pray this prayer: Jesus, I believe that you are the Son of God. Please forgive me of my sins, and come into my life and be my Savior and Lord. Teach me your ways. Help me to be quick to listen and slow to speak. Give me wisdom that I may know the truth of your Word, and bring glory to your name. In Jesus' name I pray, Amen. If you prayed this prayer, you are now in the family of God and you need to start reading your Bible. This will help you to become grounded in the Word of God. Most people go and join a church so that they can get guidance in their walk with the Lord. I was a little different, I studied the Bible for seven years before I started going to church. God knows what is best for you. Just heed His direction and don't stop walking with Him no matter what happens.

We are not trying to narrow down all of the prophecies of the end times during this study. We are trying to put a border of time around the puzzle, to help us to understand what is coming on God's plan for this age. We can then look closely at the other prophecies in the Bible and put them in the proper context. I hope this study has helped your understanding of God's complete power and authority over all things, as well as his *mo'ed* or appointed times, as your walk with the Lord Jesus continues.

APPENDIX A

2 Peter 3:8
But beloved, be not ignorant of this one thing, that one day with the Lord is as a thousand years, and a thousand years are as one day.

The chart on the following pages shows how our current calendar, of 365 days equals one year, compares with God's 1000 years equals one day calendar. God's feasts are listed with the name of each day of the week, so that we can see what God is doing in Scripture to fulfill those holidays or feasts. There are also brief descriptions of events in man's calendar to help establish the major events on the second level of time.

Day	Day of Week	Years	God's Feasts	God's Sabbath	Comments
First	Sunday	0 - 1000	Feast of Trumpets	High Sabbath	Heaven and earth are created. Light and darkness are separated. God starts creating and rests.
Second	Monday	1000 - 2000	Feast of Trumpets (Cont.)	High Sabbath	Expanse was created to separate the waters. God is still resting.
Third	Tuesday	2000 - 3000	None	None	Dry ground was created. Vegetation was started.
Fourth	Wednesday	3000 - 4000	None	None	Sun, moon and stars created.
Fifth	Thursday	4000 - 5000	None	None	Fish and birds created.
Sixth	Friday	5000 - 6000	None	None	Animals, and man are created. Year 442 of the sixth day Adam is created on God's time frame 5442. Adam was tempted. Starting now Rev. 2:10 is in effect. (See day fifteen)

Appendix A

Day	Day of Week	Years	God's Feasts	God's Sabbath	Comments
Seventh	Saturday	6000 - 7000	None	Yes	Evil runs wild through the earth. God rests. Enoch is the first person on the Sabbath year 622 from Adam. Methuselah, born in Hebrew year 687. Noah born in year 1056.
Eighth	Sunday	7000 - 8000	None	None	Earth is destroyed by the flood. Shem was 98 years old at the time of the flood. Mankind starts over with Noah's family. The flood comes 1656 years after Adam's creation. Sabbath is over and God is back to work. Four hundred years of bondage begin. Egyptian bondage is broken. First Passover is given. Moses leads Israel out of Egypt.

Day	Day of Week	Years	God's Feasts	God's Sabbath	Comments
Eighth (cont.)					The Torah is given to Israel. Israel wanders in the desert for forty years. Israel takes the promised land. The birth of Isaac, in year 2048
Ninth	Monday	8000 - 9000	None	None	King David and Solomon's reign. Time of Israel's judges. Israel splits into two kingdoms; app. Hebrew year 2830. Jerusalem falls to Babylon app. 3273
Tenth	Tuesday	9000 - 10,000	Yom Kippur	High Sabbath	Intertestamental period, last 200 years of it. God rests. Jesus comes to earth. Jesus is born app. 3754 years after Adam. Day of Atonement on God's calendar. Jerusalem is destroyed by the Romans app. year 3830. Jesus fulfills all the spring feasts. Early Christian movement. The Holy Spirit is poured out.

Day	Day of Week	Years	God's Feasts	God's Sabbath	Comments
Eleventh	Wednesday	10,000 - 11,000	None	None	Covers a.d. time frame 800 to the late 1790s (Hebrew years 4656 to 5656)
Twelfth	Thursday	11,000 - 12,000	Wedding	None	Hebrew weddings happen on Thursday. We are currently in the twelfth day. Hebrew year 5761 = 2001 on our calendar. We are now 5761 years from Adam's, creation. Hosea 6.2 After two days he will revive us; on the third day he will restore us; that we may live in his presence. The thousand-year reign of Christ starts. Evil gets worse. God shortens the evil day. Satan is bound and thrown into the pit. The beast and false prophet are thrown into the lake of fire.

Day	Day of Week	Years	God's Feasts	God's Sabbath	Comments
Thirteenth	Friday	12,000 - 13,000	None	None	The thousand-year reign of Christ ends. Satan is released from the pit. Everyone not written in the Lamb's Book of Life or the book of the wicked is released. Satan is released about 1500 years before the end of the Sabbath.
Fourteenth	Saturday	13,000 - 14,000	None	Sabbath	God's rest.
Fifteenth	Sunday	14,000 - 15,000	Sukkot	High Sabbath	Great rejoicing in heaven as the new Jerusalem is ready to come to earth. This is a High Sabbath. Feast of Tabernacles.
Sixteenth	Monday	15,000 - 16,000	Sukkot	Intermediate	Satan is thrown into the lake of fire. Anyone not found in the lambs book of Life is thrown into the lake of fire. White Throne Judgement starts.

Day	Day of Week	Years	God's Feasts	God's Sabbath	Comments
Seventeenth	Tuesday	16,000 - 17,000	Sukkot	Intermediate	White Throne Judgement ends.
Eighteenth - Twenty-first	Wednesday - Saturday	17,000 - 21,000	Sukkot	Intermediate	New Jerusalem comes to earth.
Twenty-second	Sunday	21,000 - 22,000	Shemini Azeret	High Sabbath	Jesus offers living water to the people.

APPENDIX B

The dates listed for each of the Old Testament personalities shows the possible interaction between the names mentioned. We can find the date of the flood just after Methuselah's death year 1656, and back track to the creation date of Adam. This chart also helps to show us God's sabbath, on the one thousand years is as a day calendar.

Appendix B   159

Name	age	0	100	200	300	400	500	600	700	800	900	1000	1100	1200	1300	1400	1500	1600	1700	1800	1900	2000	2100	2200
Adam	930	1									930													
Seth	912		130									1042												
Enoch	905			235									1140											
Kenan	910				325									1235										
Mehalalel	895				395									1290										
Yered	962					460										1422								
Chanoch	365							622			987													
Methuselah	969							687										1656						
Lemech	777									847								1651						
Noah	950											1056										2006		
Shem	600																1558						2158	
Arpachshad	438																	1658				2096		
Shelach	433																	1693					2126	
Eber	464																						2187	
Pele	239																		1723		1996				
Reu	239																		1757			2026			
Serug	230																		1787			2049			
Nachor	148																				1819	1997			
Terach	205																				1849		2083		
Abraham	175																				1878			2123	
Isaac	180																					1948	2048		2228
Jacob	147																						2108		2255

Grey-shows the length of each person's life from the creation of Adam. The date of the flood is 1656.

APPENDIX C

This is a Julian and Hebrew calendar from the years 2000 and 2001. The Hebrew year would be 5761. This will help you to understand how both calendars interrelate and how Jewish holidays fit into the Julian calendar.

September

Sunday	Monday	Tuesday	Wednesday	Thursday	Friday	Saturday (Sabbath)
					1 Elul September 1 Rosh Chodesh	2 Elul September 2
3 Elul September 3	4 Elul September 4 Labor Day	5 Elul September 5	6 Elul September 6	7 Elul September 7	8 Elul September 8	9 Elul September 9
10 Elul September 10	11 Elul September 11	12 Elul September 12	13 Elul September 13	14 Elul September 14	15 Elul September 15	16 Elul September 16
17 Elul September 17	18 Elul September 18	19 Elul September 19	20 Elul September 20	21 Elul September 21	22 Elul September 22	23 Elul September 23
24 Elul September 24	25 Elul September 25	26 Elul September 26	27 Elul September 27	28 Elul September 28	29 Elul September 29	1 Tishri September 30 Rosh Hashanah

October

Sunday	Monday	Tuesday	Wednesday	Thursday	Friday	Saturday / Sabbath
2 Tishri / October 1 / Rosh Hashanah	3 Tishri / October 2 / Fast of Gedaliah	4 Tishri / October 3	5 Tishri / October 4	6 Tishri / October 5	7 Tishri / October 6	8 Tishri / October 7
9 Tishri / October 8	10 Tishri / October 9 / Yom Kippur	11 Tishri / October 10	12 Tishri / October 11	13 Tishri / October 12	14 Tishri / October 13	15 Tishri / October 14 / Sukkot
16 Tishri / October 15	17 Tishri / October 16	18 Tishri / October 17	19 Tishri / October 18	20 Tishri / October 19	21 Tishri / October 20	22 Tishri / October 21 / Shemini Atzeret
23 Tishri / October 22	24 Tishri / October 23	25 Tishri / October 24	26 Tishri / October 25	27 Tishri / October 26	28 Tishri / October 27	29 Tishri / October 28
30 Tishri / October 29 / Rosh Chodesh	1 Cheshvan / October 30	2 Cheshvan / October 31 / Halloween				

November

Sunday	Monday	Tuesday	Wednesday	Thursday	Friday	Saturday / Sabbath
			3 Cheshvan / November 1	4 Cheshvan / November 2	5 Cheshvan / November 3	6 Cheshvan / November 4
7 Cheshvan / November 5	8 Cheshvan / November 6	9 Cheshvan / November 7	10 Cheshvan / November 8	11 Cheshvan / November 9	12 Cheshvan / November 10	13 Cheshvan / November 11
14 Cheshvan / November 12	15 Cheshvan / November 13	16 Cheshvan / November 14	17 Cheshvan / November 15	18 Cheshvan / November 16	19 Cheshvan / November 17	20 Cheshvan / November 18
21 Cheshvan / November 19	22 Cheshvan / November 20	23 Cheshvan / November 21	24 Cheshvan / November 22	25 Cheshvan / November 23 / Thanksgiving	26 Cheshvan / November 24	27 Cheshvan / November 25
28 Cheshvan / November 26	29 Cheshvan / November 27 / Rosh Chodesh	1 Kislev / November 28	2 Kislev / November 29	3 Kislev / November 30		

December

Sunday	Monday	Tuesday	Wednesday	Thursday	Friday	Saturday Sabbath
					4 Kislev December 1	5 Kislev December 2
6 Kislev December 3	7 Kislev December 4	8 Kislev December 5	9 Kislev December 6	10 Kislev December 7	11 Kislev December 8	12 Kislev December 9
13 Kislev December 10	14 Kislev December 11	15 Kislev December 12	16 Kislev December 13	17 Kislev December 14	18 Kislev December 15	19 Kislev December 16
20 Kislev December 17	21 Kislev December 18	22 Kislev December 19	23 Kislev December 20	24 Kislev December 21	25 Kislev December 22 Chanukah	26 Kislev December 23
27 Kislev December 24	28 Kislev December 25 Christmas	29 Kislev December 26	30 Kislev December 27 Rosh Chodesh	1 Tevet December 28	2 Tevet December 29 Eighth Day	3 Tevet December 30
4 Tevet December 31						

January

Sunday	Monday	Tuesday	Wednesday	Thursday	Friday	Saturday Sabbath
	5 Tevet January 1 New Years	6 Tevet January 2	7 Tevet January 3	8 Tevet January 4	9 Tevet January 5	10 Tevet January 6 Fast Day
11 Tevet January 7	12 Tevet January 8	13 Tevet January 9	14 Tevet January 10	15 Tevet January 11	16 Tevet January 12	17 Tevet January 13
18 Tevet January 14	19 Tevet January 15	20 Tevet January 16	21 Tevet January 17	22 Tevet January 18	23 Tevet January 19	24 Tevet January 20
25 Tevet January 21	26 Tevet January 22	27 Tevet January 23	28 Tevet January 24	29 Tevet January 25	1 Shevat January 26 Rosh Chodesh	2 Shevat January 27
3 Shevat January 28	4 Shevat January 29	5 Shevat January 30	6 Shevat January 31			

February

Sunday	Monday	Tuesday	Wednesday	Thursday	Friday	Saturday Sabbath
				7 Shevat February 1	8 Shevat February 2	9 Shevat February 3
10 Shevat February 4	11 Shevat February 5 Yom Kippur	12 Shevat February 6	13 Shevat February 7	14 Shevat February 8 Tu B'Shevat	15 Shevat February 9	16 Shevat February 10
17 Shevat February 11	18 Shevat February 12	19 Shevat February 13	20 Shevat February 14 Valentine's Day	21 Shevat February 15	22 Shevat February 16	23 Shevat February 17
24 Shevat February 18	25 Shevat February 19	26 Shevat February 20	27 Shevat February 21	28 Shevat February 22	29 Shevat February 23	30 Shevat February 24 Rosh Codesh
1 Adar February 25	2 Adar February 26	3 Adar February 27	4 Adar February 28			

March

Sunday	Monday	Tuesday	Wednesday	Thursday	Friday	Saturday Sabbath
				5 Adar March 1	6 Adar March 2	7 Adar March 3
8 Adar March 4	9 Adar March 5	10 Adar March 6	11 Adar March 7	12 Adar March 8	13 Adar March 9 Purim	14 Adar March 10
15 Adar March 11	16 Adar March 12	17 Adar March 13	18 Adar March 14	19 Adar March 15	20 Adar March 16	21 Adar March 17
22 Adar March 18	23 Adar March 19	24 Adar March 20	25 Adar March 21	26 Adar March 22	27 Adar March 23	28 Adar March 24
29 Adar March 25	1 Nisan March 26 Rosh Chodesh	2 Nisan March 27	3 Nisan March 28	4 Nisan March 29	5 Nisan March 30	6 Nisan March 31

April

Sunday	Monday	Tuesday	Wednesday	Thursday	Friday	Saturday Sabbath
7 Nisan April 1	8 Nisan April 2	9 Nisan April 3	10 Nisan April 4	11 Nisan April 5	12 Nisan April 6	13 Nisan April 7
14 Nisan April 8 Unleaven Bread	15 Nisan April 9 Passover	16 Nisan April 10	17 Nisan April 11	18 Nisan April 12	19 Nisan April 13 Good Friday	20 Nisan April 145
21 Nisan April 15	22 Nisan April 16	23 Nisan April 17	24 Nisan April 18	25 Nisan April 19	26 Nisan April 20	27 Nisan April 21
28 Nisan April 22	29 Nisan April 23	30 Nisan April 24 Rosh Chodesh	1 Iyar April 25	2 Iyar April 26	3 Iyar April 27	4 Iyar April 28
5 Iyar April 29	6 Iyar April 30					

May

Sunday	Monday	Tuesday	Wednesday	Thursday	Friday	Saturday Sabbath
		7 Iyar May 1	8 Iyar May 2	9 Iyar May 3	10 Iyar May 4	11 Iyar May 5
12 Iyar May 6	13 Iyar May 7	14 Iyar May 8	15 Iyar May 9	16 Iyar May 10	17 Iyar May 11	18 Iyar May 12 Lag B'Omer
19 Iyar May 13	20 Iyar May 14	21 Iyar May 15	22 Iyar May 16	23 Iyar May 17	24 Iyar May 18	25 Iyar May 19
26 Iyar May 20	27 Iyar May 21	28 Iyar May 22	29 Iyar May 23	1 Sivan May 24 Rosh Chodesh	2 Sivan May 25	3 Sivan May 26
4 Sivan May 27	5 Sivan May 28 Memorial Day	6 Sivan May 29 Shavuot	7 Sivan May 30	8 Sivan May 31		

June

Sunday	Monday	Tuesday	Wednesday	Thursday	Friday	Saturday (Sabbath)
					9 Sivan June 1	10 Sivan June 2
11 Sivan June 3	12 Sivan June 4	13 Sivan June 5	14 Sivan June 6	15 Sivan June 7	16 Sivan June 8	17 Sivan June 9
18 Sivan June 10	19 Sivan June 11	20 Sivan June 12	21 Sivan June 13	22 Sivan June 14	23 Sivan June 15	24 Sivan June 16
25 Sivan June 17	26 Sivan June 18	27 Sivan June 19	28 Sivan June 20	29 Sivan June 21	30 Sivan June 22 Rosh Chodesh	1 Tamuz June 23
2 Tamuz June 24	3 Tamuz June 25	4 Tamuz June 26	5 Tamuz June 27	6 Tamuz June 28	7 Tamuz June 29	8 Tamuz June 30

July

Sunday	Monday	Tuesday	Wednesday	Thursday	Friday	Saturday (Sabbath)
9 Tamuz July 1	10 Tamuz July 2	11 Tamuz July 3	12 Tamuz July 4 Independence Day	13 Tamuz July 5	14 Tamuz July 6	15 Tamuz July 7
16 Tamuz July 8	17 Tamuz July 9 Fast of Tamuz	18 Tamuz July 10	19 Tamuz July 11	20 Tamuz July 12	21 Tamuz July 13	22 Tamuz July 14
23 Tamuz July 15	24 Tamuz July 16	25 Tamuz July 17	26 Tamuz July 18	27 Tamuz July 19	28 Tamuz July 20	29 Tamuz July 21
1 Av July 22 Rosh Chodesh	2 Av July 23	3 Av July 24	4 Av July 25	5 Av July 26	6 Av July 27	7 Av July 28
8 Av July 29	9 Av July 30	10 Av July 31				

August

Sunday	Monday	Tuesday	Wednesday	Thursday	Friday	Saturday Sabbath
			11 Av August 1	12 Av August 2	13 Av August 3	14 Av August 4
15 Av August 5	16 Av August 6	17 Av August 7	18 Av August 8	19 Av August 9	20 Av August 10	21 Av August 11
22 Av August 12	23 Av August 13	24 Av August 14	25 Av August 15	26 Av August 16	27 Av August 17	28 Av August 18
29 Av August 19	30 Av August 20 Rosh Chodesh	1 Elul August 21	2 Elul August 22	3 Elul August 23	4 Elul August 24	5 Elul August 25
6 Elul August 26	7 Elul August 27	8 Elul August 28	9 Elul August 29	10 Elul August 30	11 Elul August 31	

September

Sunday	Monday	Tuesday	Wednesday	Thursday	Friday	Saturday Sabbath
						12 Elul September 1
13 Elul September 2	14 Elul September 3	15 Elul September 4	16 Elul September 5	17 Elul September 6	18 Elul September 7	19 Elul September 8
20 Elul September 9	21 Elul September 10	22 Elul September 11	23 Elul September 12	24 Elul September 13	25 Elul September 14	26 Elul September 15
27 Elul September 16	28 Elul September 17	29 Elul September 18	1 Tishri September 19 Rosh HaShanah	2 Tishri September 20	3 Tishri September 21	4 Tishri September 22
5 Tishri September 23	6 Tishri September 24	7 Tishri September 25	8 Tishri September 26	9 Tishri September 27	10 Tishri September 28 Yom Kippur	11 Tishri September 29
12 Tishri September 30						

October

Sunday	Monday	Tuesday	Wednesday	Thursday	Friday	Saturday Sabbath
	Tishri October 1	Tishri October 2	Tishri October 3 Sukkot	Tishri October 4	Tishri October 5	Tishri October 6
Tishri October 7	Tishri October 8 Yom Kippur	Tishri October 9	Tishri October 10 Shemini Atzeret	Tishri October 11	Tishri October 12	Tishri October 13
Tishri October 14	Tishri October 15	Tishri October 16	Tishri October 17	Tishri October 18 Rosh Chodesh	Cheshvan October 19	Cheshvan October 20
Cheshvan October 21	Cheshvan October 22	Cheshvan October 23	Cheshvan October 24	Cheshvan October 25	Cheshvan October 26	Cheshvan October 27
Cheshvan October 28	Cheshvan October 29	Cheshvan October 30	Cheshvan October 31 Halloween			

BIBLIOGRAPHY

The Hebrew Calendar

Joseph Good. Rosh HaShannah and the Messianic Kingdom to Come. Hatikva Ministries: 1991 Pages 51-57.

Zola Levitt. Jewish Heritage Calendar.
Zola Levitt Ministries.

Roland De Vaux. Ancient Israel; Its Life and Institutions.
Darton, Longman & Todd LTD London also published in the U.S. by The McGraw-Hill Book Co. New York. 1994. Pages 180-193, 469

Joseph H. Hertz. The Authorized Daily Prayer Book.
Bloch Publishing Company. New York 1985. Morning Service Pages 6, 272, 302

General Editor Kenneth Barker. The NIV Study Bible
Zondervan Bible Publishers. 1985. Page 1463, 1470

Ronald H. Isaacs. The Jewish Information Source Book.
Jason Aronson Inc. Northvale, New Jersey. London 1993. Pages 232-236, 261

General Editor Kenneth Barker. The NIV Study Bible
Zondervan Bible Publishers. 1985. Pages 102-103

Rabbis Nosson Scherman/Mier Zlotowitz. The Mishnah
Mesorah Publications, LTD. Brooklyn, New York 1994. Rosh Hashanah Pages 2-14

Hatikva Ministries. A Non-Jew's Guide to Jewish Sources.
Hatikva Ministries. Port Arthur, Texas 1994. Pages 28-33

Rabbi Nosson Scherman/Rabbi Meir Zlotowitz General Editors. The Art Scroll Tanach Series; Genesis. Published by Mesorah Publications, LTD. Brooklyn, New York. 1995. Pages 38-45, 54-58

The Sabbath

Rabbis Nosson Scherman/Mier Zlotowitz. The Mishnah
Mesorah Publications, LTD. Brooklyn, New York 1994. Shabbos Pages 135-149

Rabbis Nosson Scherman/Mier Zlotowitz The Mishnah
Mesorah Publications, LTD. Brooklyn, New York 1994. Eruvin Pages 1-10

Yitzhak Buxbaum. Jewish Spiritual Practices.
Jason Aronson Inc. Northvale, New Jersey. London. 1994. Pages 405-411

Lori Palatnik. Friday Night and Beyond; The Shabbat Experience Step-by Step.
Jason Aronson Inc. Northvale, New Jersey. London. 1994. Pages 3-5, 89

Ronald H. Isaacs The Jewish Information Source Book.
Jason Aronson, Inc. Northvale, New Jersey. London. 1993. Pages 174-176, 52, 84

Roland De Vaux. Ancient Israel; Its Life and Institutions.
Darton, Longman & Todd LTD London also published in the U.S. by The McGraw-Hill Book Co. New York. 1994. Pages 480-483

General Editor Kenneth Barker. The NIV Study Bible
Zondervan Bible Publishers. 1985. Page 8, 111

Rabbi Nosson Scherman/Rabbi Meir Zlotowitz General Editors. The Art Scroll Tanach Series; Genesis. Published by Mesorah Publications, LTD. Brooklyn, New York. 1995. Pages 79-86

Joseph H. Hertz. The Authorized Daily Prayer Book.
Bloch Publishing Company. New York 1985. Pages 388, 402-413

Chassidic Teachings of the Lubavitcher Rebbe Rabbi Menachem M. Schneerson and the preceding Rebbeim of Chabad on the future redemption and the coming of Mashiach. From Exile to Redemption. Kehot Publication Society Brooklyn, New York. 1992 Pages 18-20.

E.P. Steinberg. ARCO Postal Exams. Macmillan Reference USA.
A Simon & Schuster Macmillan Company New York, NY Pages 14-15.

Grant R.Jeffrey. The Signature of G-d.
Frontier Research Publications, Inc. 1996. Page 169.

The Spring Feasts

Rabbi Abraham J. Twerski, M.D. From Bondage to Freedom.
Shaar Press and the Mesorah Heritage Foundation. 1995. Pages 43-49

Raddi Eliyahu Safran. Kos Eliyahu; Insights on the Haggadah and Pesach.
KTAV Publishing House, Inc. Hobken, New Jersey 1993. Pages 139-146.

Chassidic Teachings of the Lubavitcher Rebbe Rabbi Menachem M.
Schneersonand the preceding Rebbeim of Chabad on the future redemption
and the coming of Mashiach. From Exile to Redemption. Kehot Publication
Society Brooklyn, New York. 1992Pages 18-20.

Rabbi Nosson Scherman/Rabbi Meir Zlotowitz General Editors. The Art
Scroll Tanach Series; Genesis. Published by Mesorah Publications, LTD.
Brooklyn, New York. 1995. Pages 263-264.

Hativkva Ministries. Passover Haggadah
Port Arthur, Texas. Pages 3-6

Ronald H. Isaacs. The Jewish Information Source Book.
Jason Aronson Inc. Northvale, New Jersey. London 1993. Pages 248-253

Rabbis Nosson Scherman/Meir Zlotowitz. The Mishnah
Mesorah Publications, LTD. Brooklyn, New York 1994. Pesachim Pages 5-17

Spiros Zodhiates and AMG International, Inc. D/B/A AMG Publishers
Holy Bible 1984. Pages 92-93, 1177.

Joseph H. Hertz. The Authorized Daily Prayer Book.
Bloch Publishing Company. New York 1985. Pages 788-791.

Joseph Good. Rosh HaShannah and the Messianic Kingdom to Come.
Hatikva Ministries: 1991 Pages 18-42.

Zola Levitt. Jewish Heritage Calendar.
Zola Levitt Ministries.

General Editor Kenneth Barker. The NIV Study Bible
Zondervan Bible Publishers. 1985. Page 101, 1622-1623, 1645-1646

Avraham Yaakov Finkel. The Essence of The Holy days
Avraham Yaalov Finkel. 1993. Pages 185-187

Roland De Vaux. Ancient Israel; Its Life and Institutions.
Darton, Longman & Todd LTD London also published in the U.S. by The
McGraw-Hill Book Co. New York. 1994. Pages 484-495

Josh Mc Dowell. Evidence That Demands a Verdict.
Christian Renewal Ministries, Thomas Nelson Inc. 1979.

Fred John Meldau. Messiah in Both Testaments.
The Christian Victory Publishing Co. Denver. 1988. Pages 26-27

Translated By H. Polano. The Talmud.
Frederick Warne and Co., LTD. London, England 1973. Pages 345-347.

The Fall Feasts

Fred John Meldau. Messiah in Both Testaments.
The Christian Victory Publishing Co. Denver. 1988.

Raddi Eliyahu Safran. Kos Eliyahu; Insights on the Haggadah and Pesach.
KTAV Publishing House, Inc. Hobken, New Jersey 1993. Pages 29-30.

Chassidic Teachings of the Lubavitcher Rebbe Rabbi Menachem M. Schneerson and the preceding Rebbeim of Chabad on the future redemption and the coming of Mashiach. From Exile to Redemption. Kehot Publication Society Brooklyn, New York. 1992Pages 18-20.

Rabbi Nosson Scherman/Rabbi Meir Zlotowitz General Editors. The Art Scroll Tanach Series; Genesis. Published by Mesorah Publications, LTD. Brooklyn, New York. 1995. Pages 29-45, 571, 1462-1464.

Ronald H. Isaacs. The Jewish Information Source Book.
Jason Aronson Inc. Northvale, New Jersey. London 1993. Pages 256, 238-245.

Translation and Commentary by Rabbi Matis Roberts. Trei Asar.
Published by Mesorah Publications, LTD. 1995. Pages 137-144, 197-198.

Rabbis Nosson Scherman/Meir Zlotowitz. The Mishnah
Mesorah Publications, LTD. Brooklyn, New York 1994.
Rosh Hashanah, Yoma, Succah

Joseph Good. Rosh HaShannah and the Messianic Kingdom to Come.
Hatikva Ministries: 1991 Pages 87-94, 81

Zola Levitt. Jewish Heritage Calendar.
Zola Levitt Ministries.

General Editor Kenneth Barker. The NIV Study Bible
Zondervan Bible Publishers. 1985. Pages 176-178, 1946-1950.

Avraham Yaakov Finkel. The Essence of The Holy days
Avraham Yaalov Finkel. 1993. Pages 1-12, 15, 18.

Don Stoner. A New Look at and Old Earth.
Schroeder Publishing Company. Paramount,CA 1992. Pages 106-110.

Henry M. Morris Science and The Bible.
TBN 1986. Pages 63-64.

Chaim Nussbaum. The Essence of Teshuvah; A Path to Repentance.
Jason Aronson Inc. Northvale, New Jersey London. 1993.

Rabbi Nosson Scherman/Rabbi Meir Zlotowitz General Editors. The Art Scroll Tanach Series; Ezekiel Published by Mesorah Publications, LTD. Brooklyn, New York. 1995. Pages 304, 516-524.

Rabbi Abraham J. Twerski, M.D. From Bondage to Freedom. Shaar Press and the Mesorah Heritage Foundation. 1995. Pages 21-28.

Roland De Vaux. Ancient Israel; Its Life and Institutions. Darton, Longman & Todd LTD London also published in the U.S. by The McGraw-Hill Book Co. New York. 1994. Pages 507-509

Translated by William Whiston, A.M. The Works of Josephus. Hendrickson Publishers, Inc. 1995. Book 13 Chapter 13 Verse 5.

Translated By H. Polano. The Talmud. Frederick Warne and Co., LTD. London, England 1973. Pages 347-369.

The Other Feasts

Avraham Yaakov Finkel. The Essence of The Holy days Avraham Yaalov Finkel. 1993. Pages 108-112, 123-130.

Rabbi Abraham J. Twerski, M.D. From Bondage to Freedom. Shaar Press and the Mesorah Heritage Foundation. 1995. Pages 32-34.

Roland De Vaux. Ancient Israel; Its Life and Institutions. Darton, Longman & Todd LTD London also published in the U.S. by The McGraw-Hill Book Co. New York. 1994. Pages 510-517

The Apocryphal/Deuterocanonical Books of The Old Testament. Oxford University Press. New York, NY. 1989. Pages 157-191.

Ronald H. Isaacs. The Jewish Information Source Book. Jason Aronson Inc. Northvale, New Jersey. London 1993. Pages 245-248

General Editor Kenneth Barker. The NIV Study Bible Zondervan Bible Publishers. 1985. Pages 718-730.

Joseph Good. Prophecies in The Book of Ester. Hatikva Ministrises. 1995.

Morris B. Margolies. A Gathering of Angels. Ballantine Books. New York 1994. Page 169.

Grant R.Jeffrey. The Signature of G-d. Frontier Research Publications, Inc. 1996. Page 169.

Zola Levitt. Jewish Heritage Calendar. Zola Levitt Ministries.

Translated By H. Polano. The Talmud.
Frederick Warne and Co., LTD. London, England 1973. Pages 369-372.

A Thousand Years Are as One Day

Chassidic Teachings of the Lubavitcher Rebbe Rabbi Menachem M. Schneerson and the preceding Rebbeim of Chabad on the future redemption and the coming of Mashiach. From Exile to Redemption. Kehot Publication Society Brooklyn, New York. 1992Pages 18-20.

Rabbi Nosson Scherman/Rabbi Meir Zlotowitz General Editors. The Art Scroll Tanach Series; Genesis. Published by Mesorah Publications, LTD. Brooklyn, New York. 1995.

Zola Levett. Jewish Heritage Calendar.
Zola Levitt Ministries.

General Editor Kenneth Barker. The NIV Study Bible
Zondervan Bible Publishers. 1985. Page 882, 1903.

Translated By H. Polano. The Talmud.
Frederick Warne and Co., LTD. London, England 1973. Pages 20-21.

Don Stoner. A New Look at and Old Earth.
Schroeder Publishing Company. Paramount,CA 1992. Pages 106-110.

Henry M. Morris Science and The Bible.
TBN 1986. Pages 63-64.

Hershel Shanks. Jerusalem; An Archaeological Biography.
Random House New York. 1995.

Hal Lindsey. Planet Earth 2000 A.D.
Western Front, LTD 1994. Pages 288-289.

Hal Lindsey. There's a New World Coming
Harvest House publishers Eugene, OR 1984. Pages 239-241.

John Hagee. Beginning of The End
Thomas Nelson Publishers. Nashville Atlanta London Vancouver 1996. Pages 182-186.

Grant R.Jeffrey. The Signature of God.
Frontier Research Publications, Inc. 1996. Page 185.

SCRIPTURE REFERENCES

The Hebrew Calendar
Genesis 1:3-5
Psalms 55:17
Luke 23:44
Matthew 20:5-6
Judges 7:19
I Samuel 11:11
Matthew 14:25
Luke 12:38
Genesis 1:14-16
Genesis 7:11
Genesis 7:24
Genesis 8:3-4
Genesis 8:13
Genesis 8:14
Exodus 12:2-3
Exodus 16:1
Genesis 8:13
Nehemiah 7:73 to 8:1-2
Ezra 3:1
Zechariah 8:19
Joel 2:23

The Sabbath
Genesis 2:2-3
Exodus 20:8-11
Luke 19:28-30
Matthew 21:17
Psalms 23
Matthew 12:40
Mark 15:42
Matthew 28:1
Matthew 27:46
Leviticus 25:2-5

Deuteronomy 15:1-3
Deuteronomy 15:9
Deuteronomy 15:12-14
Leviticus 25:8-11
Leviticus 25:13
Leviticus 25:14-16
Genesis 1:5
2 Peter 3:8
Psalms 90:4
Deuteronomy 19:15b
Genesis 1:1-2
Ezekiel 1:16

The Spring Feasts
Numbers 9:2-3
Matthew 21:1-11
Matthew 22:41-46 KJV
Exodus 12:12-17 KJV
Matthew 27:46a
Matthew 27:50
John 14:33-34
I Corinthians 5:6-8
Zephaniah 1:12
Romans 6:23
2 Corinthians 5:21
Matthew 26:57-58
Matthew 27:2
Luke 23:6-7
Luke 23:11
Luke 23:44
Luke 23:50-54
Exodus 13:8
Exodus 12:3-9
I Corinthians 5:7b

Isaiah 53:1
I Corinthians 11:24b
Matthew 27:26
Psalms 22:16
Isaiah 53:5b
Isaiah 53:9
Exodus 6:6-7
Leviticus 23:9-11a
Exodus 14:13-31
Genesis 8:3-4
Luke 24:1-3
Leviticus 23:15-21
Luke 24:45-49
Acts 1:4-5
Acts 2:1-13
Acts 20:16

The Fall Feasts
2 Peter 3:9
I Peter 3-9
Ezekiel 18:21-23
Ezekiel 18:30-32
Matthew 5:23-24
Zephaniah 2:1-3
Psalms 27
John 14:6
Revelation 3:5
Hosea 14:1-9
1 Thessalonians 4:16
Ezekiel 33:1-6
Ephesians 5:13-21
Isaiah 18:3
Joel 2:1
Isaiah 26:1-3

Scripture References

I Thessalonians 4:13-18
Matthew 24:36-44
Psalms 89:35-37
Revelation 7:3
Genesis 1:1
Genesis 1:5
Genesis 8:13
Isaiah 13:9-13
Zephaniah 2:3b
Psalms 27:5
I Corinthians 14:8
Joshua 6:5
Isaiah 26:16-21
I Thessalonians 4:14-18
Revelation 11:1-3
Psalms 45
Daniel 7:19-25
Leviticus 16:32
Luke 23:34
Matthew 21:1-11
Matthew 21:12-13
Psalms 98:1
Matthew 14:28-30
John 1:42
Leviticus 16:6
Matthew 21:19
Revelation 21:9b
Matthew 22:1-14
Psalms 18:28
Ezekiel 45:1
Mark 14:12-16
John 13:3-7
Mark 14:32-42
Matthew 26:58
Luke 22:54-56
John 18:15
Luke 23:13-17
Isaiah 1:8
Matthew 27:51
Matthew 27:26
Matthew 27:45-54
Matthew 28:2-4
Leviticus 23:26-32
Numbers 29:7-11
Luke 24:13-25
Luke 24:12
Revelation 5:1-5

Leviticus 23:16-32
Numbers 29:7-11
John 24:45-49
John 20-17
John 21:5-13
John 19:28-30
I Corinthians 15:42-55
Luke 2:21
Genesis 17:12
Genesis 33:16-17
Luke 2:8-20
John 8-12
Luke 1:8-9
Zechariah 14:9
Zechariah 14:16-19
Revelation 21:1-4
Leviticus 23:40
Numbers 29:2-34
Isaiah 12:3
John 7:37-38
John 8:1-11
Jeremiah 17:12-13
I Kings 8:22-24
I Kings 8:65
Luke 2:13-14

Other Feasts

Daniel 12:11-12
Revelation 11:1-3
I Corinthians 15:51-55
Ezra 3:6
Daniel 9:24-28
Nehemiah 2:1-8
I Samuel 15:3
I Samuel 15:20-23

A Thousand Years Are as One Day

Genesis 1:1-5
Psalms 90:4
2 Corinthians 12:2
Genesis 1:1-2
2 Peter 3:8
Genesis 1:6-8
Genesis 1:9-13
Genesis 1:14-19
Genesis 1:20-23

Genesis 1:24-31
Genesis 6:3
Psalm 90:10a
Genesis 2:7
Genesis 3:6
Revelation 2:10
Revelation 20:7-15
Revelation 21:1-3
Jeremiah 42:7-10
I Samuel 25:38
Daniel 1:11-14
Acts 25:6
Genesis 2:2-3
Genesis 6:5-8
Hebrews 4:1-10
Genesis 5:21-24
Genesis 7:16b
2 Chronicles 29:15-17
Genesis 7:6
Genesis 8:15-22
Genesis 21:2-3
Acts 2:1-4
Judges 11:40
Matthew 21:19-22
Joshua 1:10-11
Revelation 19:7-9
1 Thessalonians 4:16-18
Matthew 24:32-35
Hosea 6:2
Luke 21:29-33
Revelation 20:1-3
Revelation 19:19-20
Revelation 19:6
John 19:19-22
Revelation 20:7-8
Revelation 20:9
Revelation 20:11-15
Zephaniah 1:18
Revelation 20:15
Deuteronomy 1:2
Revelation 21:1-3
Matthew 3:15
Revelation 22:17

MISHNAH REFERENCES

The Hebrew Calendar
Rosh HaShanah 1:1

The Sabbath
Shabbos 7:2
Erevin all

The Spring Feasts
Pesachim 5:1
Pesachim 7:1a
Pesachim 8:3
Pesachim 8:4
Pesachim 1:1-2
Pesachim 1:3-4

The Fall Feasts
Yoma 1:1
Yoma 1:2
Yoma 1:4-5a
Yoma 3:10a
Yoma 1:6a
Yoma 1:7
Yoma 2:1b-2
Yoma 2:3a
Yoma 2:3-3:7
Yoma 4:1a
Yoma 4:2a
Yoma 4:5a
Yoma 5:3a
Yoma 5:7a

Yoma 6:2b
Yoma 7:1
Yoma 7:2
Yoma 7:4
Yoma 8:2
Succos 1:1
Succos 5:1

Other Feasts
None

A Thousand Years Are as One Day
None

GLOSSARY

Chanukah - A Hebrew feast in the month of December or January celebrating Israel's victory over the Syrians.

Earth's time frame - The regular 365 and 1/4 day year on earth.

Erev - Boundaries in Hebrew, the laws regarding traveling on the Sabbath.

Firstfruits - The first of your ripe crops, to be paid as a tithe to G-d.

Former rain - The spring feasts fulfilled on Jesus' first coming to earth, also the spring rains that fall on Israel.

God's Time Frame - The place where a day is as a thousand years. One year would equal 365,000 of our days.

Havdalah ceremony - The closing ceremony on the Sabbath that takes us into the upcoming week.

Jubilee Year - Every forty-nine years, all sold property reverts back to the original owners, the Hebrew family who was assigned this property from the twelve tribes.

Kohanim - Priests in Hebrew, more than one priest.

Kohen Gadol - The high priest in Hebrew.

Latter rain - The fall rains in Israel, and the unfulfilled fall feasts of Israel.

Midrash - Nonlegal sections of the Talmud and rabbinic books containing biblical inter- interpretations written under the spirit of G-d.

Mishkan - The tabernacle of God during the exodus from Egypt.

Mishnah - The Oral Torah or law given to Moses by God on Mount Sinai. This contains the instructions on how to perform the laws. These laws were passed down by word of mouth from father to son until 200 C.E., when the oral teachings were compiled.

Mo'ed - God's rehearsals or appointed times.

Passover - A feast to remember the blood of the lamb protecting the Israeli people fromthe plague that destroyed the firstborn of the Egyptians.

Pilgrimage festival - A feast where all of Israel must travel to Jerusalem to worship and pay tithes.

Roman watch - a three-hour period over the nighttime hours where a soldier would stand watch. There are four of these watches in a night.

Sabbatical Year - Every seven years the Israeli people are not to plant crops so the ground has a chance to rest.

Shemini Azeret - The eighth day in Hebrew, the last day of the Feast of Tabernacles.

Shofar - A wild goat-horn trumpet.

Succah - A dwelling made for livestock.

Succos - The name for the Feast of Tabernacles.

Sukkot - The Mishnah laws reguarding the Feast of Tabernacles.

Talmud - Means teaching, the Mishnah and the Gemara (commentary on the Mishnah), together in one form.

Rosh HaShanah - The Feast of Trumpets, New Years for the Israeli people.

Sabbath - The seventh day, the day G-d rests.

Teshuvah - Repentance in Hebrew.

Tracate - One of the major topics under one of the six orders of the Mishnah. (Yoma, Erevin, Shabbos, etc.)

Watch - A four hour period in the night, of which there were three for the Hebrew people.

Yom Kippur - The Day of Atonement, the holiest day of the year for the Hebrew people, the day God forgives the sins of the people.

Peace or Panic
Order Form

Postal orders: Michael Baker
P.O. Box 609
Meadview, AZ 86444

Telephone orders: 928-564-2212

E-mail orders: gtfpurchasebook@sisna.com -OR-
gtfmike@ctaz.com

Please send *Peace or Panic* **to:**

Name: _____

Address: _____

City: _____ State: _____

Zip: _____

Telephone: (____) _____

Book Price: $14.95

Shipping: $3.00 for the first book and $1.00 for each additional book to cover shipping and handling within US, Canada, and Mexico. International orders add $6.00 for the first book and $2.00 for each additional book.

Or order from:
ACW Press
5501 N. 7th. Ave. #502
Phoenix, AZ 85013

(800) 931-BOOK

or contact your local bookstore